The Handbook of
Action Learning

Action learning is one of the most prominent individual and organisational development approaches used in all parts of the world, including in over 70 member states of the United Nations. From its early beginnings in the 1970s, it has been adopted in private, public and third-sector organisations and has produced several variations. Used for leadership and management development, to support teamwork and problem-solving, and to encourage creative thinking, it can help to develop and enhance the learning capacity for individuals and organisations.

Applied as a discrete activity focused on a priority need or on new or changed roles; as a linkage between more formal programs and the workplace or blended with other elements in a program, this book distils current and previous practice and theory to provide an up-to-date guide to action learning. The book will provide readers with an understanding of action learning, including the major elements, the choice of issues, the key skills, the role of the facilitator and applications organisation-wide. It will address such important aspects as how action learning can adapt to different national and regional cultures and how it can be evaluated. It will also offer a range of resources for further and deeper understanding.

The Handbook of
Action Learning
The Go-To Source for Individual,
Organisational and Social Development

John Edmonstone

Routledge
Taylor & Francis Group

A PRODUCTIVITY PRESS BOOK

First published 2024
by Routledge
605 Third Avenue, New York, NY 10158

and by Routledge
4 Park Square, Milton Park, Abingdon, Oxon, OX14 4RN

Routledge is an imprint of the Taylor & Francis Group, an informa business

© 2024 John Edmonstone

ISBN: 978-1-032-73487-3 (hbk)
ISBN: 978-1-032-73486-6 (pbk)
ISBN: 978-1-003-46444-0 (ebk)

DOI: 10.4324/9781003464440

Typeset in Garamond
by MPS Limited, Dehradun

Contents

Introduction

The term *"action learning"* was first adopted in 1972 by Professor Reg Revans as a result of his own working progression from a purely scientific approach to organisational problem-solving (essentially a form of quantitatively based operational research) to an acknowledgement of the centrality and importance of individual and group learning and the placing of equal value on qualitative and subjective data. In a Herculean effort through books, journal articles and conference presentations he continued to proselytise action learning across the subsequent years. Revans was a product of his time (as indeed we all are) and action learning has adapted and evolved in the ensuing years, to the extent that there may now be well at least over 60 different varieties derived from Revans' original work and a growing global spread.

I met Revans twice in the UK in the late 1970s. Once in a project in the learning disabilities field at a hospital in Derbyshire and again later at the Department of Health. In the former case, he was empathetic, supportive and engaging when working closely with front-line staff. In the latter, he was acerbic and vituperative regarding the lack of vision (as he saw it) on the part of the civil servants whose supposed interest in the learning organisation in the healthcare field did not lead them to consider the adoption of action learning as a central feature of the same.

Revans would maintain that the best way to learn about action learning would be by doing action learning and this is undoubtedly true. So why another book on the topic? The world has changed greatly even since Revans' death in 2003 and so has action learning. An explosion of books, journal articles, conference papers, reports, theses and dissertations are reflected in the founding in 2004 of the international journal *Action Learning: Research and Practice* and the related bi-annual international conferences held at various locations in the UK. Hence the growing application of action learning in different contexts has led to a greater appreciation and a deeper understanding of action learning itself. For example, while there has always been a recognition that it transcends more traditional ways of learning (1), it is now accepted that it is both central to work-based development, alongside coaching, mentoring, shadowing, secondments and networking (2) and can also operate in a blended way with a variety of programmes in higher education (3). The nature of work and of work organisations has also changed significantly as the context within which action learning operates, summarised by the notion of VUCA – volatility, uncertainty, complexity and ambiguity (4).

The book comprises 15 chapters. Chapter 1 seeks to answer the question *"What is action learning?"*, while Chapter 2 describes the underlying principles. The growth of the varieties and variations of action learning are the subject of Chapter 3 and Chapter 4 explains how individuals and organisations who may adopt action learning can best prepare themselves. The centrality of the action learning set is the focus of Chapter 5 and the importance of choosing an issue or problem is addressed in Chapter 6. Chapter 7 outlines the key skills associated with action learning, while Chapter 8 uses a model to consider the personal energy (or lack of it) of set members. Anxiety is present in all organisational contexts and inevitably also in involvement in action learning and this is considered in Chapter 9. Chapter 10 deals with the importance of supporting, recording decisive actions and how action learning sets end. While Revans was sceptical about the need for a facilitator role, the subsequent development of action learning has recognised this as an important enabler, and this is the subject of Chapter 12. Chapter 3 scales up the focus from the individual in an action learning set to a whole organisation (or organisations) level and Chapter 13 explores the relationship of action learning to different national and regional cultures. Chapter 14 looks at how action learning can be evaluated, and Chapter 15 offers a range of resources for further learning.

The book can only be a snapshot of action learning at the time of publication. Action learning has evolved from its early beginnings with Revans and will continue to do so in future. With respect to Revans' legacy, a quote from the author Terry Pratchett seems apposite:

No one is finally dead until the ripples they cause in the world die away – until the clock he wound up winds down, until the wine she made has finished its ferment, until the crop they planted is harvested. The span of someone's life is only the core of their actual existence (5).

References

1. Claxton, G. (2021) *The Future of Teaching: And the Myths that Hold It Back*, Abingdon: Routledge

2. McNamara, M., Fealy, G., Casey, M., O'Connor, T., Patton, D., Doyle, L. and Quinlan, C. (2014) Mentoring, Coaching and Action Learning: Interventions in a National Clinical Leadership Development Programme, *Journal of Clinical Nursing*, 23 (17/18): 2533–2541
3. Brook, C. and Pedler, M. (2020) Action Learning in Management Education: A State of the Field Review in Higher Education, *International Journal of Management Education*, 18 (3): 1–11
4. Edmonstone, J. (2022) *Organisation Development in Healthcare: A Critical Appraisal*, Abingdon: Routledge
5. Pratchett, T. (2022) *Reaper Man*, London: Penguin

Acknowledgements

Firstly, to Reg Revans, without whom action learning would not exist and this book would never have been written. Then to Mike Pedler and Yury Boshyk for their help, advice and inspiration over many years. Thank you to all the action set members I have worked with in the UK and overseas, most especially those associated with the NHS Scotland national clinical leadership programme "Delivering the Future". You have provided insights into the personal and organisational challenges faced daily by those seeking to make positive change. Thanks to Charles Hewson for help with word processing and finally, thank you to my editor, Kris Mednansky, for her sage and supportive advice and counsel.

Author

John Edmonstone is a leadership, management and organisation development consultant with extensive experience within public services both within the UK and internationally. He has some 30 years experience of successful consultancy work in the human resource and organisation development fields within the UK's National Health Service, local government, higher and further education in the areas of leadership and management development, coaching and mentoring, evaluation research and team development.

He has worked regularly with action learning from the 1970s onwards, largely with healthcare managers and clinical professionals but also in multi-agency contexts, principally in the UK but also in Ireland, Bosnia-Herzegovina and Indonesia. He is on the Editorial Board of the international journal *Action Learning: Research and Practice* and is the author of *The Action Learner's Toolkit* (2003), *Action Learning in Healthcare: A Practical Handbook* (2011) and *Action Learning in Health, Social and Community Care: Principles, Practices, Resources* (2018), together with many journal articles on action learning. He is an Honorary Research Fellow at Liverpool Business School, Liverpool John Moores University, having previously held similar honorary, visiting and associate appointments at Leeds, Keele, Sheffield Hallam, Queen Margaret and Copenhagen Universities.

Who Should Read this Book?

There are several audiences for this book. It will be useful for senior leaders, managers and professionals who are seeking alternatives to more conventional approaches to individual and organisational development and who wish to pursue more creative approaches to the way in which challenging issues in their organisations are addressed and people are developed. Human resource development professionals are a second group who would see the book as a guide to initiating more innovative development opportunities. Academics in higher and further education looking for ways to combine work-based development with programmes leading towards qualification and accreditation are a further relevant grouping. Action learning practitioners in the private, public and third sectors who seek a state-of-the-art summary of advances in the action learning field will benefit from this distillation of recent theory and practice. Finally, action learning participants will find in the book a clear expression of the approach which will ensure a pay-off from their involvement.

Chapter 1

What is Action Learning?

Action learning is both an ethos and a method of individual, organisational and social development based upon small groups of colleagues meeting on a voluntary basis over time to tackle real problems or issues to get things done, using an appropriate balance of support and challenge, with an imperative for action, and where there is a risk of failure – reflecting and learning with and from their experience and from each other as they attempt to change things (1,2). It sees the real world and its' challenges as the most auspicious location for learning and has been described as a pragmatic and moral philosophy (3).

The above is a personal and generic definition, Revans, the progenitor of action learning, famously refused to define it, instead establishing what it is not (see below). This lack of definition allows action learning to be *"elastic"* – to flex, change and be open to influence, and as such it has been described as a *"protean practice"* (4). It is perhaps best regarded as an open field of practice, rather than any kind of functional discipline or profession, because it evolves and borrows from related fields, giving it added depth and complexity (5). As such, it is most likely incapable of being put into any kind of single fixed competency framework, because it is both facilitative and challenging and values both intuition and reflexivity.

Ethos

An ethos is a general way of thinking about learning and a framework with a set of values and beliefs relating to, in the case of action learning, learner empowerment, participation and friendship. The distinction between ethos

DOI: 10.4324/9781003464440-1

and method is not an easy one to make (6) but the ethos is essentially humanistic and emphasises the value and agency of human beings, both individually and collectively.

It involves, for example, always starting from a position of acknowledged ignorance, admitting personal inadequacy and not knowing regarding a host of personal, organisational and social challenges. It is only when we accept that we do not know what to do that we become open to learning. In situations where there are no right answers, there can be no experts to rely on. When there are no obviously right answers, we must act in order to learn.

It is founded upon honesty about self and is whole person based, encompassing feelings, thoughts and will.

It accepts that the urge to learn is stimulated by difficulties that must be overcome, and that people learn only when they are motivated to do so. People who take responsibility in any situation have the best opportunity to take actions that will make a difference.

It recognises that people's mindsets can be powerful blocks to learning, so *"unlearning"* is also important (7). The dialogue that takes place between action learning set members offers a means of interrupting and breaching well-established patterns of thinking and behaviour as redundant mindsets are re-evaluated, re-positioned and embodied in a wider repertoire of possible responses. This is not simply about forgetting, but is concerned with advancing by slowing down, stepping back and letting go from previous understanding that can limit the future. This potentially disruptive process can be experienced as discomforting, as people may see the ways in which they have even sabotaged themselves, but also potentially liberating. By admitting the importance of *"not knowing"* and *"not acting"* (effectively an emphasis on rumination and incubation), action learning creates space for new questions and possibilities to emerge. *"Sleeping on it"* can foster this and allow the unconscious mind to get to work (8).

The ethos is based upon equality of voice and on appreciating and working with human diversity through open and frank dialogue as a means of assimilating others' perspectives and working with them. It involves high levels of trust and confidentiality and the engendering of a spirit of friendship. Ultimately it involves a commitment to action and not just thought – with the aim of doing practical good in the world (9).

Method

Action learning is not a *"recipe-book"* approach but is flexible enough to be adapted to a huge variety of different settings and challenges. Common to all the variants is a set of components.

Work

The ongoing role or job of a set member, with all the real-time issues, opportunities, experiences and actions which the workplace setting offers.

Action

The centrepiece of action learning is action. There is no learning without action and no action without learning. The action to be taken serves as the vehicle that drives the learning process, promoting critical reflection and learning.

An Individual Set Member

Everyone has personal life and work experiences, preferences and styles and faces workplace and individual challenges. In action learning they voluntarily opt to be part of a peer group of people addressing similar challenges. Each set member brings with them their own context (unique work setting), characteristics (personal styles and attributes) and challenge (workplace issue, problem, challenge or question).

Issue

The specific real-time *"presenting"* or *"starting"* problem, challenge or question that the set member has previously agreed with their sponsor in their work organisation and that the set member wants to work on in both set meetings and back in the workplace. The issue will not only be important to the set member but also to their organisation – and hopefully also to other set members. The issue might deal with strategic issues (or what to do) or operational issues (or how to do it) and may well evolve and change as the work of the set progresses. It may not always be easily recognisable or explainable and often at the outset can appear *"messy"* (not neat and easily solvable). It may be marked by some sense of a repeating pattern. The intention is to achieve tangible progress within the time available. Some sets may work on different aspects of a single shared and common issue, while others may work on a variety of different issues.

Information

This is knowledge acquired by set members and generated by individual search and research and from interaction among set members. It involves facts and data in relation to the issue or question derived from policy, reports, models, books, journal articles, workshops and so on, together with information generated from set members listening carefully to each other.

The Action Learning Set

The small and stable group of between four and eight colleagues, voluntarily formed together and committed to a supportive but challenging partnership, meeting over a fixed or agreed timescale to help action to be taken on challenges to which there are no readily available answers. The set is committed to learning from the exploration of such challenges. It is a collective space for thinking and working where every set member acts as a consultant, adviser and devil's advocate to every other set member. There is no assigned leader within the set. Every set is unique because of the individual differences between the set members, their wider contexts and the challenges which they face.

Sponsor

An influential senior person who also has ownership of the set member's issue, who wants progress to be made and who has agreed with the set member that there are benefits to them from taking part in action learning. The term *"client"* is sometimes used instead of sponsor. Sometimes a sponsor may be the immediate manager of the set member, but there can also be value in the sponsor being an *"off-line"* senior person who is willing to act as a mentor and devote time to the development of the set member. The sponsor will have discussed and agreed with the set member on the issue to be addressed, will give priority to the set member's regular attendance at set meetings and will provide ongoing support and challenge at work. This might include *"opening doors"* to other parts of the organisation and/or to other organisations. The sponsor might also attend start-up, mid-point and end-point events in the set's life. The sponsor provides the set member with clarity, support and guidance.

Champion

Within a wider organisational system, there is a role for a champion (or champions) of action learning. This is an individual or group who have previous beneficial action learning experience, who can act as an advocate and broker, linking set members to key people and ensuring ongoing momentum.

Facilitator

This is the person who sets the scene, acts as an initiator, role model and catalyst for set meetings and who is particularly active in the early days of the set. Their primary responsibility is to support the learning process, including demonstrating exemplary listening and questioning skills, ensuring that everyone is engaged and managing time within set meetings. As the set matures the facilitator may take on a more occasional role.

Process

This involves examination of the problem or issue, reflection, the forming of explanations or theories and the taking of action.

What It's Not

Action learning is part of a wider growth of interest in action-based approaches to learning. It is marked by an emphasis on the people who own their problems, together with a healthy scepticism towards the viewpoints and advice given by all types of experts. There is, however, a potential danger of confusing it with other seemingly similar development approaches. So, action learning is not.

A Discussion Group

In such a group the rule is to follow the topic under discussion, but in action learning the emphasis remains on the person and the problem or issue they have focused on and brought to the set.

A Formal Meeting

Action learning sets do not have a role for a chair or convenor and where they do have an agenda it is one created only by the set members themselves. The only similarities are the existence of tight time constraints and the production of a record of decisions made and actions agreed, but the focus is around set members' issues and their need for support and challenge in addressing them.

A Seminar

In a seminar, a presentation is made based on well-prepared material for a discussion within a group. Seminar papers are concerned with the world *"out there"*, but action learning is concerned with this only insofar as it relates to set members, their context and the issue which they bring to the set. The rules for discussion in a seminar are seldom directed towards helping the seminar-giver and upon action.

A Simulation

Simulations, case studies and games have no real consequences for the actions decided upon and taken, so the degree of commitment by participants is necessarily less. There is also the possibility of unnecessary rivalry and competition. While such activities involve analysis this is typically theoretical in nature and there is no real responsibility for any decisions taken. With no real element of risk and no possibility of seeing the consequences of decisions, there is little scope for real learning. Dealing with simulations involves defusing or abstracting conflictful situations where emotionally charged and complex issues are simply analysed into *"solutions"* (10).

A Self-Development Group

Such groups are really concerned with self-discovery, but action learning is concerned with action on the learning derived from reflection on experience. The emphasis in action learning is on making a difference *"out there"*, although *"in here"* is inevitably involved in the process of reflection. Individual development can be a result of involvement in action learning but is not the central focus.

A Support Group

Such groups emphasise support only, to the exclusion of challenge, so there is a danger of a form of collusion developing – a pleasant social gathering and a holiday from the rigours of life. Action learning's emphasis on what set members will do on return to their setting avoids this.

A Blame Group

Attacking others (as *"villains"*) and blaming them for individual, organisational or social problems, while portraying ourselves as *"heroes"* is a sterile activity and unlikely to lead to any real change.

Teambuilding

A team usually has a well-defined group task and team members work for the benefit of the task, which they must address, and which is the rationale for their being together. By contrast, an action learning set works on the future actions of individual set members, as they are typically not members of an intact team but bring an issue from an idiosyncratic context.

A Taskforce or Project Team

The emphasis in action learning is as much on learning as on action. A project team's membership is completely defined by the task it undertakes and that work is driven by the intended short-term *"deliverables"*, by progress against measured *"milestones"* and by eventual desired outcomes. A project team is dissolved when the project is completed, but an action learning set may continue for as long as the members believe they are gaining something useful from the experience.

Group Therapy

This involves exploring personal issues at the expense of work-related issues. There is no aim in action learning to *"peel away"* layers of personal meaning. Talking is not regarded as being enough – action-learning participants need to make the move from intention to action. The intention is to learn from reflection on experience to take further action, so the focus is pragmatic, and the final power lies with each participant rather than the group or facilitator.

Coaching, Mentoring and Counselling

Action learning is a group process, rather than a one-to-one process. An action learning participant can expect to be listened to and receive questions aimed at helping them but should not expect personal counselling as this is not on offer. While participants may experience action learning as a conducive context for exploring personal problems and discovering underlying personal issues (which may well interact with organisational and social strands), they are less likely to find the personal therapy they might want to deal with individual psychological problems.

Professional Supervision

There are parallels between action learning and peer-group professional supervision, not least an emphasis on the need to build trust, on confidentiality, on work-focused regular meetings, the sometimes-uncomfortable nature of self-review and the encouragement for individuals to develop personal solutions to their workplace problems by challenging their own practice. The major difference, however, is the replacement of an individual professional supervisor by *"supervision"* from a group of experienced peers.

Action Research

Given the similarity of the names, action learning and action research can superficially be seen as being one and the same. Both are certainly grounded in tackling real organisational and social issues. Even though they may look broadly similar, the two have fundamentally different approaches. Action research involves a focus on improving social practice, the involvement of practitioners and stakeholders at the outset and then throughout a project and a commitment to research that proceeds in a cyclical and iterative manner (11). It is a research approach, conducted within specific and practical organisational contexts, undertaken with rigour and understanding, to generate new knowledge and to refine practice. It is deliberate, systematic, scrutinised, verifiable and made public through publication and/or oral reports. By contrast, action learning does not require that learners collect and analyse data in such a rigorous and formal manner. Action learning is a more general approach to learning, in which research is not the primary aim and the issues addressed may not involve any formal research at all. The individual is undertaking learning from experience and reflection on that experience, through discussion, question and answer, trial and error, discovery and learning from others. Such learning is therefore a group process, yet each participant draws different learning from their different experiences. Action learning is focused on learning for those directly involved in a challenge or question, whereas in action research a team of people draw collective learning from a collective experience. Action research seeks to distil wider knowledge from specific issues, to be shared with a wider audience.

Appreciative Inquiry

There is clearly a great deal of overlap between appreciative inquiry and action learning, especially the emphasis on personal agency and collaborative working, the valuing of differences and the primacy of questions. Just like action learning, the quality of the questions posed in appreciative inquiry is a key feature, but with appreciative inquiry, the emphasis is largely placed on adopting positive rather than negative questions. There are also important differences. Appreciative inquiry has its theoretical roots in social constructionism which appears potentially liberating because it posits that if things are the way they are only so because of social convention and then we can easily change them into how we would rather have them be. Action learning, on the other hand, is grounded in a critical realism view of the world as an open system with emergent properties (12). Appreciative inquiry is also effectively an action research approach targeted principally at large group change, while action learning represents a more generic approach to individual and organisational development based upon peer support and challenge within regular meetings of the action learning set. In an action learning set participants often bring individual opportunities and challenges, so that there can potentially be as many different issues as there are set members, while in appreciative inquiry the issues addressed tend to be much broader and are identified prior to the main processes. While appreciative inquiry emphasises the positives at an individual and organisational level (but principally at the latter) action learning sets are more experimental, trying things out to see if they work and seeking to learn from that. Some of the learning of set members therefore comes from addressing the negative aspects of a situation.

While action learning is not any of these approaches, it does share several features with some of them. These examples of *"good company"* to action learning have been characterised as follows (13):

- They are all dialectic, rather than didactic or classroom-based.
- They develop contextualised and useful theory rather than adopt de-contextualised and impartial theory which is uncontaminated by practice.
- They invite learners to be active participants, leading often to change in the self and in the system in question.
- They emphasise reflection-in-action, rather than reflection on action.
- Learning tends to be facilitated, rather than taught.
- They welcome the contribution of tacit knowledge to learning.
- The learning outcomes are more often practice-based, rather than academic.
- They are comfortable with tentativeness, rather than certainty.

The Originator

Reginald Revans (1907–2003) was the originator and apostle of action learning as a means of linking thinking and doing. Powerful life experiences prompted this understanding. As a small boy, his marine surveyor father received a visit from representatives of seamen after the sinking of the Titanic. Revans asked his father what learning he had derived from the investigation and his father replied, "I *learned the difference between cleverness and wisdom*". During post-doctoral studies in physics at the Cavendish Laboratory at Cambridge University he worked alongside eight Nobel Prize winners and experienced first-hand the usefulness of teamwork, collaborative thinking and the merits of having views challenged by co-workers. This experience strengthened the beliefs which form the basis of action learning. He later served as Deputy Chief Education Officer at Essex County Council and then as Director of Education at the newly created National Coal Board. In this position he began to develop an orientation towards operational research, applying a scientific approach to practical problems in the coal industry (14). In 1955 he became Director of the Department of Industrial Administration and Professor of Industrial Management at the then Manchester College of Science and Technology. He worked there for ten years, applying his approach to hospitals, schools and factories. He subsequently resigned his chair and went to work in Belgium and then internationally.

His emerging thinking revealed a journey away from its operational research origins towards an emphasis on human actions and learning as critical factors influencing personal and organisational performance. His great insight was that a rational scientific and economic approach was insufficient, and this led him towards considerations of adult learning. The term action learning first appeared in print in 1972. The 1970s, 1980s and 1990s saw Revan proselytising action learning through numerous books and journal articles, gathering as he did so, supporters of the approach and working in a wide variety of fields (15) as action learning graduated from Revans' original pioneering work to wider applications in the development of people and organisations.

What Are the Benefits of Action Learning?

Action learning offers benefits at both individual and organisational levels.

At the *individual level,* it offers real opportunities for personal growth and learning. People face real challenges which they own and are committed to making progress on them. They reflect on how their actions, personal style, motivations and values impact on others. The focus on action and review encourages people to experiment and try different approaches, thus enhancing self-awareness. The benefits include the following:

- An improved breadth of understanding, as a basis for building relationships across an organisation or organisations and hence taking action, with broadened horizons through the sharing of different perspectives.
- Protected time to reflect, leading to people who are more reflective than emotional in tense situations.
- A safe environment that enables people to consider the difficult situations they may be in and what makes a difference in such situations.
- An antidote to feelings of isolation for specialised managers and professionals.
- An opportunity to improve personal listening skills through listening and being listened to.
- A chance to express feelings as well as facts about work situations.
- An improved ability to make sense of ambiguous situations and address complex challenges.

- An opportunity to examine personal and organisational assumptions and try out alternatives that free up thinking and help to produce practical ways forward.
- An enhanced capacity to initiate change and an increased readiness to take responsibility and the initiative, resulting in people who are more action-focused and proactive.
- Enhanced self-awareness of personal impact on others, leading to increased self-confidence and thus an improved ability to work well with others in teams.
- Shared knowledge and learning and continuing support derived from a diverse range of colleagues from different functions and organisations in a personal network.
- Legitimate and protected problem-addressing time, hence development of a creative problem-solving mindset.
- Development of skills in asking powerful questions and in giving and getting personal feedback.
- Identification of personal and career development needs and means of meeting them.
- Creation and enhancement of a strong peer network.

At the **organisational level,** the benefits include the following:

- Enabling effective action to resolve difficult issues – to do things differently and improve continuously, with the production of tangible and practical outcomes.
- Encouragement of effective teamwork in terms of inter-departmental, inter-professional and inter-organisational cooperation.
- Development of leaders with a flexible approach, with an increased readiness to take responsibility.
- Enhanced political and cultural awareness, with an improved understanding of barriers and how these might be overcome.
- Learning taking place at as fast a rate as changes, helping to create an organisational learning culture.
- Complimenting other work-based developmental approaches such as coaching and mentoring.

So, overall, the intentions of action learning are as follows:

- **To make things happen**: To make useful progress on the treatment of a perplexing problem, issue, question or opportunity that had previously seemed insoluble either within an organisation or between organisations.

- ***To help people to learn how to learn***: Enabling people to deal with such problems or issues in the future, and so ensuring the transfer of helpful learning from one situation or setting to others.
- ***To help build a learning organisation***: To create the conditions in which collective learning can occur and so foster an organisational learning *"architecture"* where continuing learning and development are permanent features of organisational life, thus helping people and organisations to survive and prosper in a complex and confusing world.

Where Is Action Learning Used?

From its origins in the UK action learning is now an international phenomenon, used in over seventy member states of the United Nations in Europe, Asia, the Middle East, North, Central and South America, Africa and the Pacific (16,17).

Global corporations make use of action learning, the major names include the following:

AstraZeneca Pharmaceuticals
AT&T
Bayer
British Airways
Cathay Pacific
Daimler-Chrysler
Deutsche Bank
Dow Chemicals
Exxon
General Electric
General Motors
Honda
IBM
Johnson & Johnson
Marriott
Microsoft
Motorola
Nokia
Roche Pharma
Samsung
Shell
Siemens

Toyota
Volkswagen
Volvo

Many of these organisations are multi-nationals where Anglo-American values predominate. However, local and national cultures differ and there is not always necessarily a match (18). The issue of action learning and national and local cultures is addressed further in Chapter 13.

In the UK, major organisations using action learning include the National Health Service, the BBC, the Civil Service, local government, the John Lewis Partnership and the police. Other applications take place in a wide range of fields, including social work, integrated health and social care, the publishing, engineering and construction industries, agriculture, banking, facilities management, community development, neighbourhood improvement, teacher education, school leadership, veterinary science, higher education, the creative industries, the legal profession, public relations, food security, poverty alleviation, anger management, passenger transport, small and medium enterprises (SMEs) and international development and relief agencies.

The Range of Applications

These applications can, and often do, operate at several levels. At the level of the *individual,* action learning is conceived as a means of initiating and continuing personal and professional development which can enable individual decisions and choices regarding careers and future learning needs. Action learning has increasingly been recognised as an enabling vehicle for leadership and management development. At the level of the *group,* action learning is seen as a means of supporting team development, including the development of trust and the inculcation of relevant skills, such as listening and questioning, across professions, occupations and departments. At an *organisational* level, action learning is a valuable means of fostering collaborative working and facilitating an organisational-wide learning culture. Finally, at the *social* level, action learning makes a significant contribution to the development of social capital – the quantity and quality of the relational connections within and across organisations, networks and systems (19). There is also a related case to be made that there is another social impact because action learning helps make good citizens of a democracy by helping people to adopt an active life stance, embrace the opportunities and challenges of organisational and social change and overcome the dominant tendency to be passive towards life's pressures. As such, it creates personal, organisational and social conditions for action which are always evolving and are open-ended. In commenting on Revans' overarching social purpose for action learning Willis (20) claimed that he:

> *Saw plainly that each individual alive is affected by the clarity or dimness of our human insights. He thought it must take an egalitarian, self-organised effort of countless individuals in small groups to move institutions and societies in more collaborative and co-beneficial directions. More than this, it would take willingness to admit that we are all ignorant of the ways in which even quite simple problems interlock with one another and cause unbearable complications. Unravelling complexities takes more than fast-track personalities, infinite computer capabilities and fierce competitiveness. It takes patient, persistent, even sacrificial human endeavour – individuals united in common effort – because so many options we must consider are matters for the human heart to act upon.*

References

1. Edmonstone, J. (2003) *The Action Learner's Toolkit*, Aldershot: Gower Publishing
2. Edmonstone, J. (2018) *Action Learning in Health, Social and Community Care: Principles, Practices and Resources*, Abingdon: CRC Press
3. Burgoyne, J. (2011) Action Learning: A Pragmatic and Moral Philosophy, in Pedler, M. (Ed.) *Action Learning in Practice*, 4th edition, Farnham: Gower, 343–355
4. Brook, C., Pedler, M. and Burgoyne, J. (2012) A Protean Practice: Perspectives on the Practice of Action Learning, *European Journal of Training and Development*, 37 (8): 728–743
5. Edmonstone, J. (2011) Action Learning and Organisation Development: Overlapping Fields of Practice, *Action Learning: Research and Practice*, 8 (2): 93–102
6. Clark, E. (2009) *Action Learning within a British Business School: Meeting the Challenge and Grasping the Opportunity*, Paper presented at Organisational Learning, Knowledge and Capabilities (OLKC) Conference, Coventry: University of Warwick
7. Pedler, M. and Hsu, H-W (2014) Unlearning, Critical Action Learning and Wicked Problems, *Action Learning: Research and Practice*, 11 (3): 296–310
8. Gregory, G. (2000) Developing Intuition Through Management Education, in Atkinson, T. & Claxton, G. (Eds.) *The Intuitive Practitioner: On the Value of Not Always Knowing What One Is Doing*, Buckingham: Open University Press
9. Edmonstone, J. (2020) A Tale of Two Ethoses: Neoliberalism and Action Learning, *Action Learning: Research and Practice*, 17 (3): 259–272
10. Raelin, J. (2000) *Work-Based Learning: The New Frontier of Management Development*, Upper Saddle, NJ: Prentice-Hall

11. Ngwerume, K. and Themessl-Huber, M. (2010) Using Action Research to Develop a Research Aware Community Pharmacy Team, *Action Research*, 8 (4): 387–406

12. Burgoyne, J. (2011) Evaluating Action Learning: A Perspective Informed by Critical Realism, Network and Complex Adaptive Systems Theory, in Pedler, M. (Ed.) *Action Learning in Practice*, 4th edition, Farnham, Gower Publishing, 427–438

13. Raelin, J. (2011) The Action Modalities: Action Learning's Good Company, in Pedler, M. (Ed.) *Action Learning in Practice*, 4th edition, Farnham: Gower Publishing, 369–379

14. Revans, R. (1982) A Consortium of Pitmen, in Revans, R. (Ed.) *The Origins and Growth of Action Learning*, Bromley: Chartwell-Bratt, 39–55

15. Pedler, M., Edmonstone, J., Chambers, N., Mahon, A., Clark, E., Baxter, H., Mitchell, A. and Garlick, V. (2022) Action Learning: Resources Held in Manchester and Salford, *Action Learning: Research & Practice*, 19 (2): 12–129

16. Marquardt, M. (2011) Action Learning Around the World, in Pedler, M. (Ed.) *Action Learning in Practice*, 4th edition, Farnham: Gower Publishing, 325–337

17. Boshyk, Y. (Ed.) (2002) *Action Learning Worldwide: Experiences of Leadership and Organisational Development*, London: Palgrave-Macmillan

18. Edmonstone, J. (2019) Is Action Learning Culture-Bound? An Exploration, *Action Learning: Research & Practice*, 16 (3): 223–237

19. Pedler, M. and Attwood, M. (2011) How Can Action Learning Contribute to Social Capital? *Action Learning: Research & Practice*, 8 (1): 27–39.

20. Willis, V. (2011) Digging Deeper: Foundation of Revans' Gold Standard of Action Learning, in Pedler, M. (Ed.) *Action Learning in Practice*, 4th edition, Farnham: Gower Publishing, 71–80

Chapter 2

Underlying Principles

The Formulae

Most likely due to his scientific background Revans expressed two root ideas about action learning as scientific-like formulae. The first is

$$L > C$$

where **L** is the rate of learning and **C** is the rate of change. This means that individuals and organisations need to be able to learn faster than things change if they are to have any hope of keeping up, surviving and prospering. Organisations that continue to embody the ideas of the past are not learning. Education and training programmes that make us proficient in yesterday's methods encourage us to *"walk backwards into the future"* and do not tell us what action to take when we meet a new challenge or opportunity.

The second formula is

$$L = P + Q$$

where **L** is *learning*, **P** is *programmed knowledge* and **Q** is *questioning insight*. Learning is seen to be made up of two major elements. The first, *programmed knowledge*, comprises two elements, external and internal. External programmed knowledge is information and skills pre-packaged for use by learners, often contained in lectures, handouts, textbooks, manuals, checklists, algorithms and so on, that have been produced to capture what has been previously learned to avoid reinventing the wheel. Internal programmed

 DOI: 10.4324/9781003464440-2

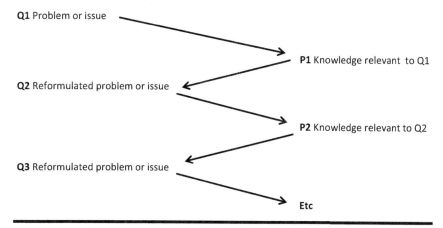

Figure 2.1   Relationship between P and Q.

knowledge is made up of personal *"mind sets"* derived from lived experience. ***Questioning insight*** is a process of active listening, questioning and reflecting, leading to review and reinterpretation of experience at the *"frontier"* edge of understanding. Questioning insight is extremely useful where there is limited degree of understanding of a problem or issue and where the issue in question is rapidly changing.

There is a danger of setting programmed knowledge and questioning insight as polar opposites. Both are necessary for effective learning. Providing programmed knowledge to learners which is irrelevant to the issue which they face can be disastrous, as is unfocused questioning insight, probably seen as a form of navel contemplation. One useful way of seeing their relationship is shown in Figure 2.1.

In Figure 2.1 a problem or issue (Q1) is explored, and it becomes obvious that some programmed knowledge is relevant to addressing this. As a result of applying this (P1) the original issue is reformulated (Q2) and in return, further programmed knowledge (P2) is applied, leading to further clarification of the issue (Q3) and so on, in a dialectical process. A problem situation will often require the application of relevant programmed knowledge, but only on a just-in-time basis.

Getting the most appropriate balance between **P** and **Q** is a major challenge. Too much **P** and not much **Q** leads to a top-down and didactic approach, while an over-concentration on **Q** at the expense of **P** means that people may end up reflecting on their reflections, without any access to **P** relevant to their situation and so simply pooling their ignorance.

Based on **L>C** the greater and faster the rate of change which individuals and organisations encounter, the quicker that **P** becomes out-of-date. So, the better the **Q** that produces new understanding of a changed situation, the better are chances of personal and organisational survival and growth. Organisations that continue to embody and express only past ideas are not learning, and this is equally true of individuals. Education and training programmes that aim for proficiency in yesterday's challenges do not help us to meet new opportunities.

Revans also provided the ***principle of insufficient mandate*** (1), expressed as *"Those unable to change themselves cannot change what goes on around them"*. This simple proposition has profound implications because it means that the starting point for change lies with each individual and that everyone, regardless of experience or status, is responsible for their own development. It also implies that the development of people is the real precondition for the development of organisations and societies. It also means that in periods of rapid and complex change a person's previous experience no matter how comprehensive and extensive is likely to be of limited relevance.

Adult Learning

Revans tempered his scientific background with insights drawn from adult learning. Learning is conceived as a natural process and not something which I *"do"*, but rather something that simply happens of itself. It is not confined to formal and structured settings like schools, colleges, universities and training centres, or to educational programmes and training courses, but is also informal in nature and so predominantly experiential, non-institutional and sometimes incidental, that is, often unintentional and a by-product of other activity (2,3). Understanding is not something that can be accumulated like knowledge and so stored in a bank. Rather it is an ongoing process better represented by the activity of *"coming-to-know"* than by a static noun (4). So, there is no such thing as *"not learning"* because we learn all the time throughout our life. Learning therefore cannot be controlled, quantified or priced, although there are clearly attempts to do so! It occurs in all domains of human experience, so learning in one domain is potentially transferable to others, dependent upon whether the organisational and social contexts are experienced as enabling or disabling.

The adult learning insights underpinning action learning are as follows:

■ ***Learning starts from not knowing***: It's only when people admit that they do not know how to proceed and are *"stuck"* or *"lost"* that they become open to learning. Where there are no *"right"* answers and no obvious ways forward and no experts available, then people must act to learn. Action learning is a practical means of sharing ignorance and acknowledging that we do not know exactly what direction to take.

■ *Learning involves the whole person*: People do not, in practice, separate their emotions from their intellect.

■ *People learn only when they want to do so*: We have an unlimited capacity to learn from our own experience, but a more limited capacity to learn from being taught. Everyone needs to work out what matters to them and what they want to do, and this enables them to make choices, act and learn as a result.

■ *The urge to learn is stimulated by the difficulties we need to overcome*: The purpose of learning is to make a difference. We learn best from real work and life challenges when applying new ideas and information and exchanging feedback with others around practical applications.

■ *People who take responsibility have the best chance of taking actions that make a difference*: Learners can cope with difficulty and complexity from the outset, if they can see that these are directly relevant to their learning.

■ *Learning is also about recognising what is already known*: Learning inevitably builds on previous experience but is not only the acquisition of yesterday's ideas but also includes trying out new and unfamiliar approaches. This means asking searching and challenging questions in the face of uncertainty, which also involves risk – the taking of actions which may or may not work.

■ *Mindsets are often powerful blocks to learning:* Human beings typically seek confirmatory evidence in order to reaffirm their existing beliefs and correspondingly tend to discard any contrary evidence. Predisposing *"mental models"* or ways of viewing the world are deeply held assumptions and generalisations made up of hopes, fears, dreams, speculations, queries, hunches, assumptions, instincts, intuitions, habits, identifications, unconscious projections, half-baked notions, social conditioning and prior training. These are not usually shared with others, are seldom explicit or necessarily logical, but do influence how we make sense of the world. They make some things possible and others not possible for us. Reviewing and revising these mindsets means recognising that a personal mindset may no longer be valid – and this can be an uncomfortable process.

■ *People learn best when they can question the assumptions on which their actions are based:* Learning increases when we are asked questions or ask ourselves questions, so that re-assessment of experience is necessary and this includes not just our knowledge and skills, but also our personal feelings and self-image.

- ***Learning and revision of mindsets is enabled in a safe and secure setting:*** This setting can contain anxieties regarding the likely impact of change on ourselves and on organisations and so creates a space for working out new ways of tackling issues.

- ***Learning is amplified when questions are posed and reflection takes place:*** Time and space to address issues, opportunities to take calculated risks, encouragement and support all enable reflection. Learning involves cycles of action and reflection. Working on *"out there"* work problems also leads to learning about personal capacity and emotional involvement. Working on *"in here"* issues of personal strengths and weaknesses leads to new experiences and growth in organisational capability. Individual learning is a visible social process which can lead to organisational change. The internal world of thoughts and feelings and the external world of action and experience are intertwined.

- ***Most people are open to learning when getting helpful and accurate feedback from those they respect, value and trust:*** Our rationality is largely determined by the surrounding social fabric. The most significant factor driving the adoption of new behaviours is the behaviour of peers (5). There is therefore much we can learn with and from others that we cannot learn alone. Support and challenge from others facing similar problems serves to stimulate our personal review processes. Learning is a social activity, helped or hindered by the network of social relationships within which it occurs.

- ***A person with an issue, question or problem is the real expert:*** The individual with the problem is responsible for it and cannot expect others to tell them what to do or solve it for them. Unless we come to realise exactly what the challenge is that we face there is little learning to be achieved. The person with the problem is the only one who has access to the relevant information and needs to ask such questions as *"Why is this important to me?"* and *"What do I really feel about this situation?"*

- ***Much learning is episodic in nature:*** Learning takes place in short bursts of intense activity that absorb the learner's attention. The pace and intensity of learning lessens when the immediate purpose has been achieved and people then resort to a much slower pace of learning before a further question, issue or challenge is stimulated which demands resolution. Learning is a situated activity, so what people learn, the pace at which they do so, and the depth and quality of understanding are all related to the circumstances in which they live and work.

■ *All learning involves personal transformation:* Learning opens new possibilities within human relationships. Through learning people can transform their sense of who they are and the possibilities within their lives, so can provide them with a deeply personal measure of how they have changed.

Learners can adopt either a surface or deep approach to learning. In the *surface approach* (which is typical of much traditional learning) the learner is simply trying to gather information and retain it for the short term in their memory. By contrast, in the *deep approach*, the learner is intent on understanding an issue and with making connections between that experience and new ideas. It is longer-term learning and involves understanding and internalising, so is more *"real"* in the sense that it is unlikely to be forgotten (6). This is not new – Aristotle distinguished between what he called *episteme* or *"knowing that"* – theoretical knowledge embodied in concepts and models – and *techne* or *"knowing how"* – pragmatic and context-dependent understanding (7). More recently, Alimo-Metcalfe and Alban-Metcalfe suggested that the competence approach in education and training only addressed *"learning that"* at the expense of learning with others, or *"learning how"* (8). Action learning fosters the deep approach, knowing how and learning how.

Research on learning (9) has identified four distinct modes regarding the way that it is used:

■ *Replicative*: This is where learning is prepared and packaged for use in situations marked by routine and repetitive tasks that call for little or no personal discretion. People learn to implement through being taught the *"right"* way to do things through given rules and procedures (see below regarding single-loop learning).

■ *Applicative*: Here the emphasis is on translating learning into prescriptions for action in a range of different situations. The emphasis is on improvement and working out how something that worked in one setting can be applied in a different one (see below regarding single-loop learning).

■ *Interpretative*: This comprises both *understanding* (seeing things from different perspectives) and *judgement* (a sense of purpose, a feel for appropriateness and flexibility based on personal experience) (see below regarding double-loop learning).

■ *Associative*: Learning in intuitive and semi-conscious ways, often involving the use of metaphors and images (see below regarding double-loop and triple-loop learning).

Most traditional learning is concerned solely with the Replicative and Applicative modes, and this tends to focus on what has been called ***explicit knowledge*** (10) or what we can *"tell"*. It is knowledge codified into formal, systematic language and communicable to others through documents, instructions, graphs, diagrams and any medium that can be stored and transmitted. It has been called *"book learning"* – recorded objective, rational and theoretical knowledge of universal truths, applicable not just in the *"here and now"* but also in the *"there and then"*. Once articulated and written down and codified it then becomes a type of commodity, to be protected by patents and other legal formulae.

By contrast, Interpretive and Associative learning are concerned with ***tacit knowledge***, which is embedded deep in the individual or collective subconscious, expressing itself in habitual or intuitive ways of doing things – those things that are done without conscious thought or effort. It is subjective understanding gained by practical involvement in the world and is both personal and context-specific. It includes our mindset mental models (the paradigms, perspectives and beliefs that guide our actions) and our action knowledge (our skills, craft and know-how). It therefore also includes our feelings, hopes, wishes, dreams and ambitions. Such learning is not easily reportable since it is deeply rooted in action and involvement in a specific context. It is hard to formalise and communicate and is probably more extensive than explicit knowledge because what is expressed in words and numbers may only be the tip of the iceberg. So, people may be knowledgeable in what they do, but they may not have the facility to say what it is they know (11).

Action learning does not see a false dichotomy between the two but accepts the co-existence and partnership of explicit and tacit knowledge, and so potentially covers the whole range. Explicit knowledge is, of course, the world of **P** and there is a continuous process of turning some tacit knowledge into explicit knowledge through *"raids on the inarticulate"*. Once the tacit has been made explicit, new tacit knowledge is built grounded in meaningful, purposeful and relevant action and resultant experience.

The differences between explicit and tacit knowledge are shown in Table 2.1.

And the differences between traditional learning and action learning are shown in Table 2.2.

Compared with traditional learning, the relationship between theory and practice is reversed in action learning. Theory is created through reflection and dialogue to explain and clarify experience, rather than learned before experience is attempted. This results in the lack of any defined *"curriculum"* or predetermined specification of knowledge, which in turn makes evaluation of action learning somewhat challenging, because what is learned is not specified

Table 2.1   Explicit (Technical) and Tacit (Practical) Knowledge

Explicit (technical) knowledge	Tacit (practical) knowledge
Typically codified and written	Typically expressed in practice and learned only through experience
Based on established practice	Based on established practice modified by idiosyncratic technique
In accordance with prescription	Loosely, variably, uniquely. In a discretionary way based on personal insight
Used in clearly defined circumstances	Used in both expected and unexpected circumstances
To achieve an envisaged and familiar result	To achieve an indefinite or novel result
Emphasis on routine – method, analysis, planning	Emphasis on non-routine – variety, invention, responsiveness
Focus on well-defined problems	Focus on poorly defined problems

Table 2.2   Differences Between Traditional Learning and Action Learning

Traditional learning	Action learning
Input-based. Content predetermined and scheduled	Output-based. Content is responsible and opportunistic
Classroom-based	Workplace-based
Knowledge orientation	Action/application orientation
Understanding demonstrated by description and explanation	Understanding demonstrated by action
Teaching by informing and explaining	Encouragement of grappling, thinking and acting
Emphasis on reading and writing	Emphasis on dialogue talk
Learning primarily individual-focused	Learning equally individual, group, organisation and social-focused
Passive – little choice/control by learner	Active – significant choice/control by learner
Learning is memorising	Learning is exploring
Theoretical – disembodied from real-life concerns and contexts	Practical – embedded in real-life concerns and contexts
Focus on achievement	Focus on investigation, experiment, achievement and development
Past-orientated	Present/future-orientated

in advance or in any detail, if at all, and may not even be what was originally intended. This means that action learning is very challenging to traditional learning (12) and much management and leadership education (13). Action learning also challenges the power relationship in the learning situation. Neither the action learning set facilitator nor the set member's employing organisation are wholly in charge because, compared with traditional learning methods, accountability for what is learned remains largely with the individual learner.

Traditional learning seeks to provide learners with generic knowledge and skills but leaves the challenge of transferring that to the learner's setting and to the learner themselves. This is known as the *"learning transfer problem"* (14). In these contexts, there may be few rewards (and perhaps even some penalties) in attempting something new or different. As a result, initiatives often *"fizzle out"* and this ***vicious learning sequence*** is shown in Figure 2.2.

Action learning instead embodies a ***virtuous learning cycle*** where learning is focused on improving personal, organisational or social effectiveness, with the result that learning is perceived as relevant and easier to apply. Resulting payoffs then increase enthusiasm for learning. This is shown in Figure 2.3.

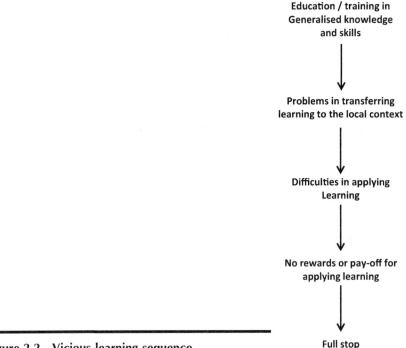

Education / training in
Generalised knowledge
and skills

Problems in transferring
learning to the local context

Difficulties in applying
Learning

No rewards or pay-off for
applying learning

Full stop

Figure 2.2 Vicious learning sequence.

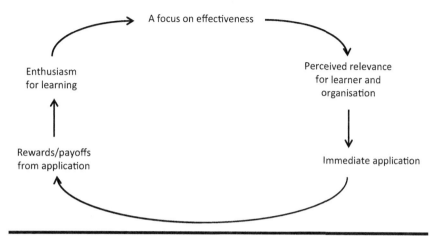

Figure 2.3   Virtuous learning cycle.

Puzzles and Problems

Problems, challenges, issues and questions come in a wide range of shapes and sizes. Action learning distinguishes between *puzzles* and *problems*. The former are like crossword puzzles, with *"right"* and *"wrong"* answers and *"best"* solutions. They are individual, organisational and social embarrassments which could be resolved by the application of **P**. By contrast, problems are complex, rather than just complicated, dynamic, rather than static, novel and often recalcitrant and intractable. In effect, puzzles and problems are what have been called *"tame"* and *"wicked"* (15).

Puzzles/Tame Issues

- Can be described in a clear and simple statement.
- Exist where there is limited uncertainty about the issue.
- Are where the roots of the issue are either already known or are easily discernible.
- There is broad agreement amongst interested parties about what *"success"* would look like.
- Do not fundamentally change over time.
- Respond well to rational planning and management tools.
- Previous experience and practice with the same or similar issues are useful guides towards a resolution.
- Solutions are transferable to other settings and contexts.
- It is clear when a solution has been reached.
- Objective evaluation can take place,

Problems/Wicked Issues

- Are characterised by a high degree of uncertainty.
- Interact with other issues, so cannot be addressed in isolation.
- Will appear as *"fuzzy"* – unclear, incomplete and possibly contradictory.
- What *"success"* might be is difficult to define.
- Cross organisational boundaries and managerial and professional hierarchies.
- Seem to defy rational analysis and planning.
- Involve multiple perspectives on what the issue is and what the right way forward might be.
- Are strongly related to the context in which they exist.
- Previous experience and practice are little help toward resolution.
- Progress will require individuals and organisations to change mindsets and behaviour, to choose between contradictory values and learn new ways of working.
- Resolution of the issue might create further problematic issues.

Action learning can address both puzzles/tame issues and problems/wicked issues. In the former case, tangible and concrete outcomes can be easily identified and achieved. In the latter case the diversity of set membership and the asking of powerful and penetrating questions and the challenges which this entails means that action learning is well-suited to addressing such issues (16,17). It is also possible that what is presented as an issue and seems, at first sight, to be a puzzle or a tame one, can be re-viewed and re-framed as emerging from a wicked one, by working on the originally presented one. This is likely to be the case when examining such aspects as how people work together (or not); their different roles, priorities and ways of working and the degree of cooperation and information-sharing.

Balancing Learning and Task Achievement

In most organisations, there exists an *"action-fixated non-learning cycle"* (18) which operates for most people for most of the time. People view a situation and in a *"rush to judgement"* almost immediately devise an explanation or theory which forms the basis of any action they take to address that situation. Reviewing experience is either forgotten or short-circuited to get things done quickly in a culture of *"busyness"*. The ability to promote decisive and directive action is highly prized and asks such questions as *"How much can we get done"* and *"How quickly can we arrive at a decision?"* This orientation is marked by feelings of urgency and has been described as a *"hurry sickness"* (19). This is shown in Figure 2.4.

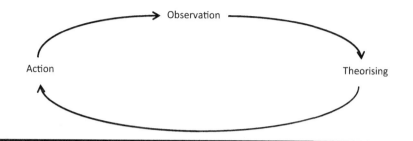

Figure 2.4   Action-fixated non-learning cycle.

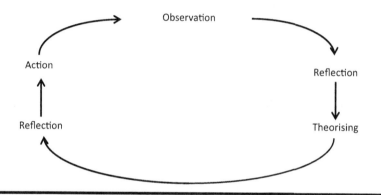

Figure 2.5   Action learning cycle.

Taking action in this way is not the same as acting and then reviewing the experience of doing so with colleagues – and learning from it. A second activity cycle – of learning – is necessary and is shown in Figure 2.5.

This cycle emphasises the importance of reviewing past and present experiences and of identifying what has been learned from it, as the basis for planning what is to come next. Balancing the tension between achievement (action) and clearer understanding (learning) can only be achieved by giving equal attention to processes of review, reflection and the devising of next steps.

Single- and Double-Loop Learning

Single-Loop Learning

With single-loop learning (20), the key questions which are being addressed are *"Are we doing what has been specified?"* and (by implication) *"Are we doing things right?"* These are essentially "how?" rather than *"why?"* questions because with

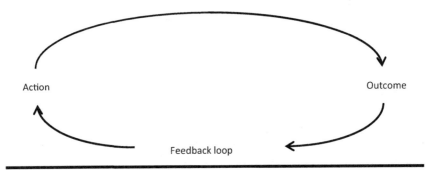

Figure 2.6 Single-loop learning.

single-loop learning people are not required to consider and modify any of the existing standards, expressed as organisational rules or guidelines, but simply to follow them, because they are taken as simply being given. The aim is instead to ensure that everyone follows such rules and guidelines and performs to the formally agreed, and such taken-for-granted, or implicit, common standards, so that any errors or deviations from the standards can be quickly detected and then corrected.

More complex thinking and questioning by individuals are deemed not to be necessary because the expectation is only to identify and then to correct any such deviations from the prescribed standards (21). Causality (the relationship between cause and effect) might be observed but is not addressed. Single-loop learning therefore essentially focuses on tame problems (22) and these are largely operational and routine in nature and so are principally concerned with organisational efficiency and with looking *"inwards and downwards"* in a hierarchical sense and with a focus on issues of control and performance (18). These are *"difficulties from which escapes are thought to be known"* (1).

Single-loop learning is most everyday learning and is essentially adaptive and tactical in nature which only seeks to narrow the gap between actual and desired positions. It is therefore aimed at improving existing performance at an increasing rate by seeking more efficient ways of producing existing goods or delivering existing services. Single-loop learning is illustrated in Figure 2.6.

Double-Loop Learning

Double-loop learning asks *"Why?"* and *"So what?"* questions such *as "Are we doing the right things?"* and *"Have we even specified what are the right things to do?"* Existing norms and standards are called into question if there is a possible better way of seeing and doing things. The aim is to identify, understand and, where necessary, challenge and change the existing mental frameworks, norms,

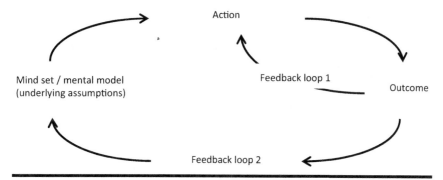

Figure 2.7 Double-loop learning.

policies and rules which underlie everyday actions and routines (23) by processes of reflection on existing patterns and trends. It encourages people to question assumptions, raise the existence of conflicts and change their minds because of feedback. It is clearly less comfortable than single-loop learning and so potentially might stimulate conflict. It represents *"out-of-the-box"* thinking and doing and can potentially lead to a redefining of goals, norms, policies, procedures, roles and structures. It is both strategic and generative in nature and so is effective in dealing with complex, non-programmable issues – so is highly useful in addressing wicked problems (16,24). Double-loop learning is shown in Figure 2.7.

Triple-Loop Learning

Some have posited the possibility of triple-loop learning which addresses the question *"How do we even decide what is right?"* This is conceived of as learning, which is additional to, and at a higher level than, single-loop and double-loop learning. At this level the essential principles upon which an organisation is founded and then operates now come under consideration with a view to the development of new principles, upon which the organisation can potentially develop further. It is therefore concerned with underlying purposes, principles or paradigms. Yet there is a profound difference of opinion as to whether such triple-loop learning can even be facilitated or engineered in work organisations, and hence institutionalised. Bateson (25) suggests it cannot be achieved through any conscious and instrumental means, not least because it involves a shift in understanding which lies beyond the reach of language. Yorks and Marsick (26) concur with this view, noting that such generative learning is unpredictable and so not controlled or controllable and so, as Bateson proposes, from an organisational standpoint is inherently risky. While single-loop and double-loop learning appear to be concerned with rational knowledge and to operate at cognitive and affective levels, triple-loop learning appears to be non-instrumental, may exist beyond language and is recursive – so seems to be ultimately concerned with the development of the wisdom of individuals, rather than of organisations.

Inferring and Mindsets

During a human lifetime our mindsets of attitudes and beliefs become reinforced by our selective attention to events. Attention is most often paid to confirming, rather than disconfirming data. Most of the time this is a natural and helpful process which helps people to avoid information overload and a continuous reappraisal of people and situations. As a result, we operate for much of the time based on biases and prejudices. No two people typically experience the same event in the same way because our use of such mental *"short-cuts"* can be unhelpful.

Problems usually occur from not testing our attributions about other people's behaviour. It becomes more difficult to be explicit about our thinking processes, especially in situations we experience as threatening. When things go wrong, we may attribute to others our own weaknesses, assuming that we all fail for the same reasons. We try to protect ourselves and others by not telling them about the negative attributions we make about them, and this is considered the *"right"* thing to do. However, by avoiding confrontation and leaving such attributions untested they can become self-fulfilling prophecies, even if inaccurate. From our experience, we then select certain data to which we add meanings which are based on our prior personal and cultural experience and these form the basis of the assumptions we make and then the conclusions we draw. These conclusions enable us to adopt beliefs about the world upon which we base our actions. This is a *"self-sealing"* process, as the beliefs which we then adopt affect the data selected the next time. Only by breaking this reinforcement, by examining and then challenging the assumptions, can deeper learning take place – and action learning offers just such a means for this to happen.

References

1. Revans, R. (2011) *The ABC of Action Learning*, Farnham: Gower Publishing
2. Claxton, G. (1981) *Wholly Human: Western and Eastern Visions of the Self and its Perfection*, London: Routledge & Kegan Paul
3. Marsick, V. and Watkins, K. (1997) Lessons from Informal and Incidental Learning, in Burgoyne, J. & Reynolds, M. (Eds.) *Management Learning: Perspectives in Theory and Practice*, London: Sage, 27–39

4. Peat, D. (1996) *Blackfoot Physics*, London: Fourth Estate
5. Pentland, A. (2014) The Death of Individuality, *New Scientist*, 5 April
6. Marton, F. and Saljo, R. (1976) On Qualitative Differences in Learning: 1. Outcome and Process, *British Journal of Educational Psychology*, 46: 4–11
7. Aristotle (2004) *The Nicomachean Ethics*, London: Penguin
8. Alimo-Metcalfe, B. and Alban-Metcalfe, J. (2008) *Engaging Leadership: Creating Organisations that Maximise the Potential of Their People*, London: Chartered Institute of Personnel and Development
9. Eraut, M. (1994) *Developing Professional Knowledge and Competence*, London: Falmer Press
10. Polanyi, M. (1966) *The Tacit Dimension*, London: Routledge & Kegan Paul
11. Pleasants, N. (1996) Nothing Is Concealed: De-centring Tacit Knowledge and Rules from Social Theory, *Journal for the Theory of Social Behaviour*, 26 (3): 233–255
12. Claxton, G. (2021) *The Future of Teaching and the Myths That Hold It Back*, Abingdon: Routledge
13. Parker, M. (2018) *Shut Down the Business School: What's Wrong with Management Education*, London: Pluto Press
14. Huczynski, A. (1978) Approaches to the Problem of Learning Transfer, *Journal of European Industrial Training*, 2 (1): 26–29
15. Edmonstone, J. (2014) On the Nature of Problems in Action Learning, *Action Learning: Research & Practice*, 11 (1): 2–41
16. Crul, L. (2008) Solving Wicked Problems through Action Learning, *Action Learning: Research & Practice*, 11 (2): 215–224
17. Grint, K. (2008) Wicked Problems and Clumsy Solutions: The Role of Leadership, *Clinical Leader*, 1 (1): 54–68
18. Garratt, B. (2000) *The Learning Organisation: Developing Democracy at Work*, 3rd edition, London: HarperCollins Business
19. Friedman, H. & Booth-Kewley, S. (1987) Personality, Type A Behaviour and Coronary Heart Disease: The Role of Emotional Expression, *Journal of Personality and Social Psychology*, 53 (4): 783–792
20. Argyris, C. (1976) *Increasing Leadership Effectiveness*, New York, NY: Wiley
21. Kuhl, S. (2019) *The Rainmaker Effect: Contradictions of the Learning Organisation*, Princeton, NJ: Organisational Dialogue Press
22. Rittell, H. and Webber, M. (1973) Dilemmas in a General Theory of Planning, *Policy Sciences*, 4: 155–169
23. Cope, J. (2003) Entrepreneurial Learning and Critical Reflection: Discontinuous Events as Triggers for "Higher-level" Learning, *Management Learning*, 34 (4): 429–450
24. Pedler, M. and Hsu, S-W. (2014) Unlearning, Critical Action Learning and Wicked Problems, *Action Learning: Research and Practice*, 11 (3): 296–310
25. Bateson, G. (1973) *Steps to an Ecology of Mind: Collected Essays in Anthropology, Psychiatry, Evolution and Epistemology*, London: Paladin
26. Yorks, L. & Marsick, V. (2000) Organisational Learning and Transformation, in Mezirow, J. (Ed.) *Learning as Transformation*, San Francisco, CA: Jossey-Bass, 89–100

Chapter 3

Distinctions and Differences

Revans never prescribed exactly how action learning should be done, so there is no single agreed definition of action learning and therefore no single way of doing it. The definition offered in Chapter 1 is personal to the author and for working purposes only – and there are certainly others. This preference for avoiding definition reflects the root sources of action learning practice and, as a result, attempts have been made to ascribe them to different *"schools"* – Scientific, Experiential, Critical Reflection and Tacit/Incidental (1). As action learning has grown and spread, it has metamorphosed into a range of different varieties and variations, at the last count some 62. Perhaps a useful analogy of action learning is that of a tree, where *"Classical"* action learning forms the trunk, and the evolving varieties form the branches. The main versions and varieties are:

Mainstream or "Classical" Action Learning

This is probably closest to what Revans originally developed (2). It is best located in the *"cognitive map"* (or Lyotard Triangle) (3) shown in Figure 3.1.
    This framework is based on three positions (4).

Speculative

Learning for its own sake, unconcerned with any application to practical issues and concerned largely with theoretical rigour.

 DOI: 10.4324/9781003464440-3

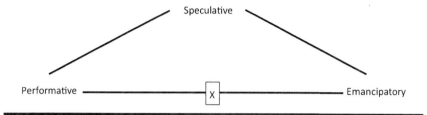

Figure 3.1 A cognitive map of action learning.

Emancipatory

Learning that individually and collectively helps to overcome oppression and to attain the highest human potential, so with a strong moral element and concerned with the holistic development of the person in the world.

Performative

Learning that helps with action in the world that resolves problems and produces better goods and services. Significantly concerned with improving and enhancing performance.

This original version of action learning is positioned at point X between the Performative and Emancipatory positions and seeks to combine improving organisational performance with personal development, seeing no contradiction between them. It involves set members meeting face-to-face and addressing personal and organisational challenges.

Self-Managed Action Learning

Although current good practice usually involves the use of a facilitator working with an action learning set, Revans himself was sceptical about the need for such an individual, especially on an ongoing basis. This variant (5) seeks to dispense with such a role. Here the term facilitator is often replaced with that of *"set manager"* and the role is undertaken by the set members themselves. Set meetings are much more structured and less free form than with the mainstream version. There are two rounds of time slots – one is retrospective and focuses on reflecting and looking back to learn the lessons of experience – and one is prospective, looking forward to identifying actions needed to move matters forward.

Self-managed action learning is less common because

■ Often set members and their organisational sponsors expect that a facilitator role is necessary.

- There is often a lack of understanding at the outset among set members as to what the action learning process entails.
- There is a need to help set members to get to know each other and develop trust at an early stage.
- There is usually a lack of self-facilitating skills among the set members.
- There seems to be a need for someone to be held responsible for helping the learning process.

Nevertheless, self-managed sets are sometimes a viable option, particularly where the set membership is already experienced in action learning, but to be successful this requires

- A high personal commitment from all set members to attend the set meetings and to share the work of facilitation.
- Clear agreement among set members about the format which is to be followed for set meetings and clarity over the roles which are adopted.
- A high degree of honesty in reviewing each set meeting to avoid collusion or to ignore or avoid discussing possibly unhelpful behaviour.

Sets which do feature a facilitator can evolve towards a self-facilitating existence. The aim would be to make the role as redundant as possible as quickly as feasible. The process of the facilitator leaving the set would need to be explicit from the outset, so the facilitator might advise set members at an early stage *"We will need to decide at what point my presence will not be needed"*. This would be a joint decision. The facilitator might also ask set members to review the role and how it is working out after an agreed number of set meetings. If the role becomes less and less necessary a facilitator might then attend set meetings by invitation only – as and when the set membership feels it might be necessary and helpful, for example, when an impasse has been reached and the set feels *"stuck"*.

Virtual Action Learning

While the origins of this variant began in the 1990s and so predate the COVID-19 pandemic, this version of action learning was certainly accelerated by its existence. It offers an alternative to the face-to-face interaction which other sets provide. It is conducted in a virtual environment using collaborative communications technology and comes with both advantages and disadvantages, benefits and challenges. While earlier virtual approaches involved email and text messaging, audio and video recording, the advent of firstly, Skype, and latterly Zoom and Microsoft Teams, has ensured the growth of the virtual approach (6,7).

The ***advantages*** in adopting the virtual approach include

- Sets can cover a wide geographical area and even be international in nature, allowing for much greater diversity in set membership.
- It can make action learning more accessible to people who may not otherwise be able to attend face-to-face meetings.
- Significant savings can be made in both travel time and costs. Set meetings can take place without the time, financial and environmental costs associated with travelling.
- The non-physical presence and sense of anonymity compared with face-to-face meetings can potentially foster more openness, help to establish personal identities and speed up the development of trust and good working relationships.
- Listening seems intensified and it becomes easier to concentrate on what is being said without the need to constantly maintain eye contact, as in face-to-face sets. Listening skills are sharpened and trust developed more quickly than in face-to-face sets.
- Responses are therefore more thoughtful than in faster face-to-face dialogue.
- Voice is more *"visible"* in intonation, tone, inflection, speed and silences.

The ***disadvantages*** include

- The non-physical presence and anonymity present a difficulty for some set members.
- The complexity of the technology which is not always familiar to participants and may not be easy to use. Calls may be dropped, and sound distorted.
- People may not give it the seriousness and commitment which they would an in-person meeting.
- There may be prospects of set members being interrupted by interventions from work colleagues or senior people.
- Finding a quiet and safe place to participate might be challenging for some people. The background environment may therefore be noisy and distracting.
- Confidentiality may be easier to breach.
- It may not be possible to read body language.
- Where the set is too large it can be challenging.

Virtual action learning is heavily dependent on the skills of the facilitator, and these operate at two levels. At the ***macro-level*** the facilitator must create the initial conditions necessary to set up virtual set meetings and this involves the time and effort required in identifying set membership, preparation for the technology and the setting-up of virtual meetings. At the ***micro-level*** the facilitator needs to acquire the resources, skills and processes necessary to run virtual set meetings, managing both the technology and the process. The major common challenges are telephone interruptions, more *"urgent"* matters and the distracting and disrupting influence of powerful senior people. Further problems may be the ability of all set members to connect to good Wi-fi and the question of digital literacy – is everyone able to successfully use the technology?

Of importance in working virtually is ***"netiquette"*** – the rules of behaviour which amplify the value of the approach. They include

- The need to find a quiet room where the set member will not be distracted, for the duration of the set meeting.
- The facilitator needs to use clear language, to check for understanding and to provide breaks where appropriate.
- Different individual learning styles need to be considered.
- Aiming for only one person to speak at a time, yet accepting some interruptions where there is a need to develop trust and spontaneity.
- Seeking to apportion equal time to each person in discussing and exploring the issue.
- If someone seems quiet during a session, aiming to bring them in.
- When someone is reviewing possible action to take, noting down any suggestions and highlighting them.
- Keeping to the timings agreed.
- Providing notes of the session afterwards.

Sets may commence on a face-to-face basis and then continue forward on a virtual basis – a hybrid arrangement. A possible danger of virtual action learning sets relates to the fact that some organisations may see them as both a cheaper alternative than face-to-face set meetings and solely as a technical process for problem-solving, thus at least limiting the possibilities for personal and organisational development (8).

Business-Driven Action Learning

In this variant the issues which set members work on are not chosen by them but are organisationally derived and reflect an organisation's current and future strategic and operational priorities (9). This approach emphasises the integration of a business and results-focused orientation with individual development and team effectiveness as set members pursue measurable results. Exploration of organisational issues or ideas generation around an issue or opportunity relating to a business challenge feature strongly. Based on the "Classic" set model for facilitation, the facilitator's role is a flexible one. The approach requires major support from senior leaders and managers to set up and then to sustain. Provided that set members are familiar with the issues offered, they might well have chosen them anyway, but while this variant is superficially attractive there are also risks that:

■ What the organisation offers as a *"presenting"* issue may have roots in a more challenging area, where the organisation might not want to go.
■ A set member might come up with an *"unacceptable finding"* – a conclusion at odds with the conventional wisdom in the organisation which challenges established interests or involves the deployment of resources that are unobtainable.
■ Action learning becomes regarded as simply a tool or means to an end.

In terms of the framework shown in Figure 3.1, business-driven action learning is closer to the Performative position.

World Institute for Action Learning Approach

Originated in the USA but increasingly operating internationally, this approach involves *"certified"* coaches and master coaches using a very structured process, associated with team coaching. There is a strong problem-solving orientation regarding business challenges with claims of return on investment regarding organisational, leadership and team development projects. Like Business-Driven Action Learning, this version is closer to the Performative position in Figure 3.1.

Critical Action Learning

Critical action learning (10–12) asserts that all action learning takes place in a context which includes elements which may be unspoken and unconscious and will remain that way unless a facilitator takes an active role in surfacing them. Such elements include the power dynamics within the set, the related power relationships within an organisation, the relationship between set members and the facilitator and the emotions and experiences of the set members themselves.

Hence, critical action learning invites set members to be aware of the power dynamics that they are experiencing, creating, representing and enacting. The emphasis is not only on the empowerment of the individual set member, but also on the ways that learning and action are supported, but also avoided and prevented, both within sets themselves and within organisations, through power relations. It assumes that the latter are an inevitable and integral part of action learning and may be exemplified by individual set members' risk-averse behaviour within a set, by collective defensiveness and denial and by set members' unconscious compliance with taken-for-granted organisational habits, norms and expectations.

The distinguishing features of critical action learning are as follows:

- An emphasis on the ways that learning is supported, avoided and/or prevented through power relations.
- The linking of Q (questioning insight) to complex emotions and to unconscious processes and relations.
- An emphasis on collective, as well as individual, reflection on organisational, political and emotional dynamics.
- Reflection which is critical of taken-for-granted assumptions regarding the social and political forces which provide the context for work and organisations.
- A more proactive facilitator role.

Critical action learning is challenging of existing power relations within organisations and hence can be an uncomfortable experience for set members, their sponsors and their organisations. It offers a means of correcting an unquestioning acceptance of a dominant ideology and values, where people and organisations are unwilling, unlikely and seemingly unable to question such a perspective. It addresses the danger that action learning runs a risk of capture by corporate interests for use simply as a tool – a means of effecting improvement in organisational performance while maintaining a status quo of dominance and control (13). As such, it is closer to the Emancipatory position in Figure 3.1.

Critically Reflective Action Learning

This is a process which seeks to go beyond critique to work towards social justice outcomes by fostering insight into personal theories-in-use, identifying constraints of assumptions, habits and ideology and emphasising the making of ethical choices (14). This places critically reflective action learning close to the Emancipatory position in Figure 3.1.

Action Reflection Learning

This variant developed from work by educators and consultants at Lund University in Sweden in the 1970s and the creation of the MiL Institute under the guidance of Lennart Rohlin in 1977. The term itself was not adopted until 1987. Based upon Revans' principles and directly influenced by him it involves sixteen elements and ten learning principles. It strongly emphasises the importance of reflection in developing and implementing projects, together with the development of personal theories. It incorporates a facilitator role (called a *"learning coach"*), focuses on team projects, rather than individual problems, is flexible with the number and duration of sessions and sees a role for *"experts"* – which Revans was sceptical of, to say the least (15,16). It is close to the Performative position in Figure 3.1.

Co-Development Action Learning

Developed in Canada in the 1990s and active across the French-speaking world, mainstream action learning was a significant source of inspiration for co-development, defined as an open, collaborative and appreciative group approach to reflection on action which seeks to build a community of practice where members support and learn from each other. It features some guiding principles, a structured method and clearly defined roles (17).

Auto Action Learning

This approach is intended to supplement the membership of an action learning set for an individual set member. It involves the use of a mentor outside of the set providing an opportunity for reflection, learning and the devising of planned actions. This is intended to speed up learning and act as a motivator to apply experience from elsewhere to the issue. It also serves to build the empowerment of the set member. It involves a series of parallel relationships (set membership and mentoring) which serve to reinforce each other. The use of such a structured format focuses attention both retrospectively (on learning achieved) and prospectively (on forward action) and thus keeps a focus on motivation, learning and review (18).

Project Action Learning

Developed jointly by academics and practitioners in China and Australia, this approach has a strong organisational, problem-solving, goal-driven and project management-based orientation. It is based on four "pillars" – policy and strategy, organisational learning facilitation, performance management and technology resources and infrastructure, with the intention of developing a learning organisation (19). The facilitator role is an interventionist one and the approach is closer to the Performative position in Figure 3.1.

Positive Action Learning

This approach has been developed by Jeff Gold and Alaa Garad in their book *"The Learning-Driven Business: How to Develop and Organisational Learning System"* (20). It comprises a strategy and a range of tools for creating a learning-driven business or learning organisation. Strongly practitioner-based and recipe-orientated the intention is to provide an accessible workbook, and this positions the approach closer to the Performative area, as seen in Figure 3.1.

Emancipatory Action Learning

While this is not a recognised *"school"* of action learning it is most reflective of the work of the southern hemisphere-based Action Learning and Action Research Association (ALARA) and closer to the Emancipatory position in the framework shown in Figure 3.1 (21). Action learning is used in combination with action research under the heading of Participatory Action Learning and Research (PALAR) and is especially concerned with social change. More details about ALARA are shown in Chapter 15.

Network Action Learning

This is action learning applied to sustainable improvement and innovation in collaborative inter-organisational networks aimed at strategic improvement, with problem-solving at its core, and is largely focused on unknown or wicked problems (22).

Anticipatory Action Learning

This is an integrative process that relies on a central thread of conversation among a variety of participants, from multiple perspectives, concerned with a project. It has been described as action research modified by foresight (23,24).

Blended Action Learning

This takes place where action learning is used alongside a range of other approaches as part of a development programme which may, or may not, be accreditation and qualification-based. It sits alongside other activities such as coaching, mentoring, workshops, and online virtual learning platforms. It is *"blended"* with these approaches as a means of contributing towards the overall intended outcomes of a programme. Used especially on leadership and management development programmes, the applications include (25):

- A planned and timetabled activity interwoven with other aspects of a programme, with the action learning set either ceasing at the end of the programme or being encouraged to continue in a self-managed fashion for as long as set members derive benefits.
- An activity introduced towards the end of a programme with the anticipation that programme participants would form sets as a way of continuing their development, so bridging the potential divide between the programme and the work setting.
- A discrete development activity, neither relying on, nor continuing the momentum of, a formal programme, but often focused on support and challenge for people in newly emergent roles.

References

1. Yorks, Y., O'Neil, J. and Marsick, V. (1999) Action Learning: Theoretical Bases and Varieties of Practice, in Yorks, L., O'Neil, J. and Marsick, V. (Eds.) *Action Learning: Successful Strategies for Individual, Team and Organisational Development, Advances in Human Resources, No. 2*, San Francisco, CA: Berrett-Koehler, 1–18
2. Willis, V. (2004) Inspecting Cases against Revans' Gold Standard of Action Learning, *Action Learning: Research & Practice*, 1 (1): 11–27
3. Burgoyne, J. (2011) Action Learning; A Pragmatic and Moral Philosophy, in Pedler, M. (Ed.) *Action Learning in Practice*, 4th edition, Farnham: Gower, 343–355
4. Pedler, M., Burgoyne, J. and Brook, C. (2005) What Has Action Learned to Become? *Action Learning: Research & Practice*, 2 (1): 49–68
5. Bourner, T. (2011) Self-Managed Action Learning, in Pedler, M. (Ed.) *Action Learning in Practice*, 4th edition, Farnham: Gower, 113–123
6. Dickenson, M., Burgoyne, J. and Pedler, M. (2010) Virtual Action Learning: Practices and Challenges, *Action Learning: Research & Practice*, 7 (1): 59
7. Aspinwall, K., Pedler, M. and Radcliff, P. (2018) Leadership Development through Virtual Action Learning: An Evaluation, *Action Learning: Research & Practice*, 15 (1): 40–51

8. Keating, M. (2022) Reflections on Virtual Action Learning Sets, *Action Learning: Research and Practice*, 19 (2): 198–199

9. Boshyk, Y. (2011) Business-Driven Action Learning Today, in Pedler, M. (Ed.) *Action Learning in Practice*, 4th edition, Farnham: Gower, 141–152

10. Trehan, K. (2011) Critical Action Learning, in Pedler, M. (Ed.) *Action Learning in Practice*, 4th edition, Farnham: Gower, 163–171

11. Vince, R. (2011) Learning in Action or Learning Inaction? Emotion and Politics in Action Learning, in Pedler, M. (Ed.) *Action Learning in Practice*, 4th edition, Farnham: Gower, 415–426

12. Hauser, B., Rigg, C., Trehan, K. and Vince, R. (2023) How to Facilitate Critical Action Learning, *Action Learning: Research and Practice*, 20 (1): 116–131

13. Willmott, H. (1997) Critical Management Learning, in Burgoyne, J. & Reynolds, M. (Eds.) *Management Learning*, London: Sage, 161–176

14. Roche, C. (2022) Decolonising Reflective Practice and Supervision, *Philosophy of Coaching: An International Journal*, 7 (1): 30–49

15. Rohlin, L. (2011) Action Reflection Learning, in Pedler, M. (Ed.) *Action Learning in Practice*, 4th edition, Farnham: Gower, 125–139

16. Turner, E. and Rimanoczy, I. (2008) *Action Reflection Learning: Solving Real Business Problems by Connecting Learning with Earning*, Mountain View, CA: Davies-Black Publishing

17. Paquet, M., Sabourin, N., Lafranchise, N., Cheshire, R. and Pelbois, J. (2022) Codevelopment Action Learning during the Pandemic: Findings from Two Online Co-Learning and Co-Creation Events: Twenty Codevelopment Action Learning Sessions Were Held Simultaneously for 148 People from Nine French-Speaking Countries, *Action Learning: Research & Practice*, 19 (1): 19–32

18. Learmonth, A. and Pedler, M. (2004) Auto Action Learning: A Tool for Policy Change: Building Capacity across the Developing Regional System to Improve Health in the North East of England, *Health Policy*, 68 (2): 169–181

19. Law, K. and Chuah, K. (Eds.) (2020) *Project Action Learning (PAL) Guidebook: Practical Learning in Organisations*, Cham, Switzerland: Springer Nature

20. Garad, A. and Gold, J. (2021) *The Learning-Driven Business: How to Develop an Organisational Learning Ecosystem*, London: Bloomsbury Business

21. Zuber-Skerritt, O., Wood, L. and Kearney, J. (2020) The Transformational Potential of Action Learning in Community-Based Research for Social Action, *Action Learning: Research & Practice*, 17 (1): 34–47

22. Coughlan, P. and Coghlan, D. (2011) *Collaborative Strategic Improvement through Network Action Learning: The Path to Sustainability*, Cheltenham: Edward Elgar Publishing

23. Stevenson, T. (2002) Anticipatory Action Learning: Conversations about the Future, *Futures*, 34 (5): 417–425

24. Burke, R. (2021) Anticipatory Action Learning, Leadership, Strategy and Foresight: Creating a Successful Future While Enhancing Results Today, *Journal of Futures Studies*, 25 (3): 85–92

25. Edmonstone, J. (2022) Action Learning and Healthcare, *Action Learning: Research & Practice*, 19 (3): 248–250

Chapter 4

Preparing for Action Learning

Assessing the Climate and Culture

Typically, organisations tend to turn to action learning when:

- They need to tackle difficult problems or deal with a new and challenging situation.
- There is a need to develop people who can manage successfully change and uncertainty.
- Jobs, roles and organisations are changing.
- New collaborations, networks and alliances must be created.
- Both personal and organisational development is required.
- Traditional course-based education and training programmes are seen as being inappropriate and ineffective.

However, there will be a need to assess exactly how ready they are to commence with action learning. The extent of organisational readiness will be a major factor influencing the eventual success of action learning for both organisations and individuals. The context or setting will be more (or less) conducive to successful outcomes. Readiness is rooted in a range of questions:

- Does the organisation really want to do it?
- Is the organisation in a place where it is ready to do it?

DOI: 10.4324/9781003464440-4

- Will the issues chosen involve set members in real and significant change?
- Are these issues unknown enough to need imaginative and creative ways forward?
- Will the issues expose set members to a range of different perspectives and ways of working and learning?
- Is what is being considered feasible and realistic in terms of the timescale, resources, experience and skills available?
- Are the risks of failure high enough to stimulate action without being threatening?
- Are senior people really committed to the success of action learning?
- Does the organisation (or organisations) have the power and will to make the changes arising from the action learning process?

Ideally, an organisation should combine openness and support with enough challenge to the status quo to stimulate learning and change. Not all organisations will necessarily be in such a place. Those with a strong *"training"* culture may not feel comfortable with action learning, because their default tendency will be to constrain uncertainty and establish order through curricula, courses and techniques (1). By contrast, being in a better place would involve:

- Support and commitment from senior organisational levels.
- A willingness to address system-wide issues and examine *"wicked"* as well as *"tame"* problems (2).
- A tolerance for uncertainty and ambiguity.
- An embracing of diversity as a stimulus for creativity.
- A degree of discretion and freedom of action for individuals (3).

Assessing the degree of organisational readiness can be aided by some helpful tools. The ***Organisational Fitness Ranking*** (4) provides useful questions for an organisation considering adopting action learning and directs thinking towards whether it should be used to consolidate existing areas of strength or address more problematic issues. It also helps to identify the different perceptions of individuals and groups on such matters. The ***Organisational Readiness for Action Learning Questionnaire*** (5) helps an organisation rate itself against a set of learning organisation criteria and offers a guide to the likely value of action learning. Readiness is seen as existing when sufficient challenge is balanced with an appropriate degree of openness and support. The readiness conditions are often most prevalent early in an organisation's life cycle because when it becomes older, larger and more complex much of the original natural learning ability can be lost.

More generally, the personal and organisational factors which enable and disable successful outcomes from action learning can be identified.

Enablers

- A match between the climate of the organisation and the assumptions underlying action learning. This implies a dissatisfaction with conventional and didactic approaches to personal and organisational development.
- A linkage between the use of action learning and other relevant and supportive activities.
- An appreciation of the wider context, including how an organisation works, how influence is brought to bear and how this can be activated and mobilised.
- Influential people within the system who take close and supportive interest in what sets do and help them to grapple with issues.
- Sponsors of set members who, either by personal experience of action learning or understanding and support of the underlying assumptions, prioritise attendance at set meetings over organisational crises.
- Problems, issues and questions that are challenging enough.
- Set membership which is significantly voluntary and diverse.
- Preparation for set meetings – undertaking what was previously agreed and being ready to report on it.
- Regular attendance at set meetings.
- Active participation in set meetings, listening and responding to what is said.
- A willingness by set members to take a long hard look at themselves.
- A capacity to be open and responsive.
- The use of open, awareness-raising and elaborating questions in the set to help set members address issues and their ownership of them.
- Making best use of time within set meetings.

Disablers

- A mismatch between the organisation's culture and the assumptions underlying action learning.
- Action learning as an *"island"* activity, divorced from more strategic concerns, so free of connections to set members' contexts.
- Lack of senior figures who understand and support action learning.
- Sponsors who don't support action learning, due to lack of personal experience of it or with values at odds with it, resulting in perfunctory support and interruptions by local organisational crises.
- Set members sent to sets as a reward or a punishment.
- Unbalanced set membership.

■ Non-attendance or *"spotty"* attendance at set meetings, together with no follow-through on agreed actions.
■ Non-appropriate issues brought to the set.
■ Passive attendance at set meetings.
■ Non-preparation for set meetings.
■ Expectation of a *"magic bullet"* to solve problems.
■ Lack of balance between support and challenge in the set meetings.
■ Tale-spinning, time-wasting and game-playing.
■ Imposing *"advice"* on others, scoring points and demonstrating supposed cleverness.
■ Unhelpful questions.
■ Breaching confidence.

Taster Events

One way of familiarising people with the possibilities of action learning is through taster events where they can get a flavour of what it entails. Such an event could last for a day or a half-day and might involve

■ A presentation on the basic concepts underlying action learning.
■ An opportunity to experience some of the dynamics of a set, possible through the Slow-Motion Questioning Exercise shown in Chapter 15.
■ A chance to explore a range of options including intra-organisational or intra-professional sets, multi-organisational and/or multi-professional sets, multi-agency sets, themed sets around an issue or kick-start sets, where facilitation is provided only for a limited number of early meetings.

Commitment

At an early stage the degree of commitment necessary for success should be clear on the parts of:

■ *A set member.* Commitment is displayed by identifying and agreeing on an issue to be worked on in and between set meetings, accepting that this may evolve or change – and then regular attendance at set meetings, preceded by any necessary preparation (not least because non-attendance has a negative impact on those who do attend), and by reporting on progress made on the chosen issue. Also, by listening carefully to the questions asked by other set members and agreeing actions to be taken back in the workplace. There will also be a need to actively listen to the situations of other set members and to support and challenge them where necessary. There may also be informal communication with other set members between meetings. The workplace is where action on the set member's issue takes place and involves reflecting on the success or otherwise of such actions, in preparation for describing this at the next set meeting. While there are time and energy implications of being a set member, the more an individual invests in the process, the more powerful the impact, both in practical actions and learning.

■ *Sponsor:* The sponsor may need to become a little more informed about action learning and attend a start-up and endpoint event and will need to realise that a set member's involvement may be unlike their attendance on more conventional programmes. They will need to work with the set member to identify a real, significant and challenging issue that will involve implementation as well as diagnosis and accept that the original issue chosen may evolve further. They will need to meet with the set member between set meetings. There will be important payoffs to the sponsor, including increased inter-functional and inter-departmental information-sharing; improved teamwork across departmental boundaries; a reduction in *"silo"* working and greater role clarity, especially in situations where new roles are created or emerge. Sponsors need to be aware of such potential payoffs at the outset.

■ *Organisation:* The whole organisation needs to understand that previous perplexing issues will now be addressed and that this may possibly turn out to be uncomfortable for some. The positive outcomes are likely to be an increase in the capability to change, generate new knowledge and improve performance; the generation of a culture of continuous improvement and a situation where the rate of learning is at least as rapid as the rate of change which organisations experiences.

References

1. Pedler, M. and Abbott, C. (2013) *Facilitating Action Learning: A Facilitator's Guide*, Maidenhead: McGraw-Hill/Open University Press
2. Rittel, H. and Webber, M. (1973) Dilemmas in a General Theory of Planning, *Policy Sciences*, 4: 155–169
3. Jacques, E. (1976) *A General Theory of Bureaucracy*, London: Heinemann
4. Pedler, M. (2008) *Action Learning for Managers*, 2nd edition, Aldershot: Gower Publishing
5. Pedler, M. and Aspinwall, K. (1996) *Perfect Plc? The Purpose and Practice of Organisational Learning*, Maidenhead: McGraw-Hill

Chapter 5

The Action Learning Set

The action learning set is the small group which is the vehicle for the learning process. It is how set members work out and pursue their own actions in the workplace and learn from that experience through processes of review, reflection and planning. The set is concerned with:

- Helping set members learn from the issues they are addressing, so they can increasingly challenge their own and others' assumptions.
- Diagnosing the nature of the challenge and then going on to implement practical ways forward.
- Moving into uncharted territory where problems are unfamiliar, rather than areas where set members are already experienced.

Membership

Sets are of two types:

- ***Stranger set***: Here the set members do not come from the same workplace, so it is easier to facilitate because set members are not involved in each other's organisations and so are able to offer disinterested listening.
- ***In-house set***: This involves set members from the same organisation and is more problematic, involving more risks, but with a greater potential pay-off. The possible danger is that the set may prefer to resort to a general

       DOI: 10.4324/9781003464440-5

discussion as a means of *"learning inaction"* (1) or avoid the surfacing and addressing of significant issues – *the "elephant in the room"*.

Set Formation

The formation of a set is a vital process and there are several ways in which a set may be formed. The key criteria are:

- *Interest*: Involvement in a set should, wherever and whenever possible, be voluntary because the personal motivation of set members is powerful in sustaining their effort over the life of the set.
- *Level of challenge*: This should be broadly similar for all set members.
- *Mix of roles and organisations*: This is important to ensure a diversity of experience and background and to promote the potential for cross-system learning and networking.
- *Diversity of personal style*: A rich mixture can be created by the personal skills of set members, together with their professional and organisational experiences and styles. Enough contrast is needed to provide the *"grit in the oyster"*, although too much diversity may make it difficult for the set to establish a shared sense of identity.
- *Equality*: It is helpful if a set shares a broadly common age range or work experience, with broadly the same responsibility level, career progression and experience, though this can be difficult to achieve in practice. No one set member should feel out of their depth. In an in-house set senior people should probably not be in the same set as their staff especially where there may be dominant personalities and where a status-ridden and hierarchical organisational setting may exist.
- *Gender mix*: A balance should be sought, as far as possible, between male and female set members.
- *Geography*: In face-to-face sets this is important for travel and meeting purposes.
- *No personal animosity*: Action learning is not conflict resolution, so those with a *"history"* between them would most likely be uncomfortable in each other's company, would be less likely to be open and would colour the overall tone for other set members.

Sets can be formed around a specific need, such as people taking up a new role or tackling a new initiative and this is straightforward and easily managed but may remove the element of choice on the part of potential set members and so lessen the degree of diversity and *"stretch"* available.

Self-Selection of Set Membership

There is a process for forming sets out of a larger group which relies upon an iterative process to arrive at flexible criteria for self-selection of set members. The rules for adopting this process are:

- All sets must be **finally** formed at the same time.
- Conversations all take place in one room with everyone taking part.
- Sets need to be formed by the end of an agreed time period.

People must consider their own criteria for forming or joining a potential set and will need to engage in dialogue with other potential set members. A series of conversations in pairs, trios and larger groups across the agreed time period can lead to a more *"natural"* emergence of sets. A facilitator can assist this process by offering questions that might be addressed such as:

> *"Do I want to work with people I already know? Why is this?"*
> *"Should I aim to join a set with people I've never met? Why is this?"*
> *"Should I consider the professions/occupations and organisations of the others? Why is this?"*
> *"Should I aim to work with someone whose behaviour I find challenging? What are the advantages and disadvantages of doing this?"*
> *"Who will really challenge me? Why do I want this?"*
> *"Who will support me? Why do I want this?"*
> *"Does the issue I bring to the set have any implications for my choice? Why is this?"*

This approach enables people to create their own learning environment from the outset. It does take time to achieve and may possibly provoke feelings of uncertainty and even anxiety for some – the age-old question of *"Will I be picked for the team?"* Nevertheless, the pay-off lies in the sense of ownership which set members then have in relation to the set which they opt to be a member of.

Alternative Set Groupings

There are three alternative configurations for set groupings:

- *Horizontal sets*: These are sets made up of people working at a similar organisational position or status level within one, or across several, organisations. This is a configuration adopted by most sets. Shared experience and common ground help to reduce barriers and encourage greater levels of trust. However, if set members' perspectives are so familiar to each other it may be more difficult to challenge shared views.

- **Vertical sets**: These sets are made up of people drawn from different levels within the same function or profession/occupation. They demonstrate a strong level of commitment from the setting concerned and promote a concept of equality of contribution from everyone. They encourage a full spectrum of viewpoints on issues and provide a ready-made means of communication between the levels concerned, so enhancing the likelihood of subsequent action. However, if there are pre-existing over-hierarchical or dominant relationships then this grouping may stifle set members' input and create difficulties for them in communicating ideas and concerns.
- **Hybrid sets**: When there are several sets running across an organisation or organisations there may be an advantage in also creating another set made up of representative members of the *"regular"* sets to focus on what continuing learning is being achieved and action taken across the entire system, rather than only on the specific issues addressed within the sets.

Questions Regarding Set Membership

There are useful questions to consider by organisations and facilitators when considering potential set membership and these include:

> *"Is there anyone missing from the proposed membership who could really contribute to the work of the sets?"*
> *"Will every set member be allowed to attend set meetings, or will they be subject to pressure from more senior people and/or colleagues for doing so?"*
> *"Will the proposed configurations produce all-female, all-male or mixed gender sets, and if so, does it matter?"*
> *"What will be the maximum and minimum number of set members for the set to work effectively?"*

Answers to these questions will vary according to the focus of the sets, the organisational setting and the overall intention in using action learning.

Location and Venue of Set Meetings

This is important for face-to-face set meetings and depends upon travel distances and times for set members. A quiet, adequately heated and well-ventilated room is the basic requirement, with comfortable chairs, preferably of the same design and arranged in a circle or rectangle. Access for the less able should be considered at the outset, as should transport and/or parking facilities. Refreshments and meal arrangements must be clear and flipcharts, pens, paper and so on easily available. There should be no interruptions or distractions. A single *"neutral"* venue might be chosen or alternatively set members might take it in turn to host set meetings.

When considering the venue, the issue of boundary protection is important. Set members need to feel that they are working in a private, safe and supportive environment where they can address their concerns. The set acts as a holding environment or transitional space in which the set members can handle their inevitable anxiety, so the extent to which the set is able to exclude the immediate demands and pressures of the work setting and create a space which is truly the set's own for the duration of the set meeting, without any work-related intrusions will be a major key to success.

Duration of Set Meetings

The larger the set membership, the longer meetings will last, and vice versa. A set should, as a rule, allow at least 45 minutes per participant at each set meeting, and there may be value in adding a further 30 minutes to the overall time for slippage and/or comfort breaks. While no one set is typical, a meeting involving five set members might last for 3–4 hours, but a meeting involving seven or eight members would most likely last a whole day.

Frequency of Set Meetings

Sets need time to work properly, and this will vary depending on the needs of the set members and the emerging dynamic. Because of the cycle of action and reflection, sets feed on the work that goes on between set meetings. Thus, the life of the set depends to a great extent on the issues which the set members bring to the meetings.

Sets run for a range of different periods, often for up to 6 or 12 months, but there does need to be a clearly defined endpoint. The gap between meetings should not be so close that attendance and time are problematic, not so far apart that momentum, as sense of continuity, mutual confidence and trust are lost. Set meetings need to be planned, programmed and booked well in advance and key holiday dates and work pressure peak periods considered to ensure maximum attendance.

Ground Rules

Early in the life of a set ground rules need to be established to guide and govern the behaviour of set members and the facilitator, to allay any fears about what might happen in the set and to model shared responsibility. The creation of such a code of conduct acts as a guardrail and makes it less likely that set members will be disappointed or frustrated. Ground rules are of two types:

Practical ground rules, which cover such things as:

- *Attendance and punctuality*: The importance of being there and being on time.
- *Life-expectancy of the set*: Over what time period is it anticipated that it would meet?
- *Frequency and duration of set meetings*: How often will the set meet and for how long on each occasion? Will there be breaks and if so, how many and when?
- *Format of meetings and time allocation*: What format will the meeting have and how much airtime will be available?
- *Each person to have equal voice and time.* Everyone has a right to this, but don't necessarily have to take it.
- *No use of jargon.*
- *Recording*: Will notes on actions to be followed up taken, by whom and how will these be shared? Will someone be responsible for taking notes? Will learning diaries or learning journals be used?
- *Conflicts of interest:* Are there any?
- *Exchange of contact details*: To enable contact between set meetings.

Behavioural ground rules, addressing such matters as:

- *Commitment and priority*: The necessary self-discipline to attend set meetings and to undertake agreed workplace actions.
- *Confidentiality*: The personal stays in the room. Often set members agree to share topics with others providing that specific identifying details are omitted. While everyone is likely to subscribe to confidentiality in principle, it will be important to agree on what this means in practice. It cannot ever be absolute, but agreeing on limits and when and how information might be shared outside the set will be important. Clarity here allows set members to decide what to disclose in set meetings. If in doubt, perhaps leave it out.
- *Stay fully present* during questions and dialogue, so no texting or emailing.

- **Respect**: For others' views, which means being non-judgemental. Being empathetic to others' contexts and circumstances, guarding against assumptions and judgements.
- **Ensure equal opportunity** to participate and sufficient time to engage with questions and dialogue before moving on.
- **Timekeeping and punctuality**: Keeping to both the external time boundaries (starting and finishing on time) and the internal ones (the airtime for each set member).
- **One person speaks at a time**: No talking-over or interrupting
- **"I" language**: Saying *"I"*, rather than *"one"*, *"we"*, *"they"* or *"you"*.
- **"And" rather than "but"**: Beginning a sentence in response to a statement shows that two divergent views can co-exist without seeking to demolish the other.
- **No "shoulds" and "oughts"**: These are effectively commands and should be avoided.
- **Clarity**: It is OK to check out assumptions and ask questions if something is not understood.
- **Allow silence**: This gives people time to think before asking questions and responding to them and conveys the sense that listening is taking place. Resist the urge to fill the silence.
- **Allow expression of feelings**: Feelings are facts too.
- **Recognise and appreciate** that honesty, effort and intent are more important than how succinctly we express things.
- **Resist the temptation to** ask for advice or ask for a preferred solution.
- **The right to say "No"**: It is OK to decline to respond to a question or challenge.

The exact number of ground rules is not important and varies from set to set. A further important ground rule to agree is that all ground rules are open to renegotiation and new ground rules can be agreed at any time that the set feels it is necessary.

Time and Process

Set members usually come from a work environment where the default position is to *"shoot from the hip"* – to aim to fix things quickly, achieve certainty and agreement in the context of intense and sometimes repetitive work events. This *"solutionising"* is marked by continuing feelings of urgency, so the overriding goal is to reach quickly for decisions – a form of *"hurry sickness"* (2) where people feel chronically short of time, try to perform each task faster and get anxious and flustered when encountering delay (3). Ambiguity and paradox are avoided in favour of certainty, with a preference for instant solutions and an overwhelming *"bias for action"* (4). This has been described as hitting the target but missing the point.

By contrast, working in the set involves slowing down, listening and reflecting and this is liberating for some but difficult for others who find that the tempo of the set does not match that of their work environment. Adjusting to a different way of working together can feel awkward for some, like a right-handed person signing their name with their left hand. What happens in the set is not a debate or a discussion, but a dialogue where meaning flows between people and leads to greater and shared understanding – a form of exploration and joint inquiry. Assumptions can be surfaced; deeper appreciation can be gained, and unseen possibilities identified. Through such a shared conversation different perceptions and connections can emerge and insights can be achieved.

Resistance to Learning

Some people may resist learning when it involves personal change and challenges their current view of the world and themselves. Action learning means surrendering a degree of stability to embrace something new and uncertain, so it is not surprising that resistance may be triggered. This may emerge as:

■ Dissonance between action learning and more traditional and familiar education and training approaches. What may seem like a lack of structure and an emphasis on collective learning may generate feelings of confusion and conflict.
■ Questioning deeply rooted values and assumptions can be disturbing as people examine beliefs that have governed much of their lives and careers.
■ Group dynamics within the set such as diversity of set membership or different levels of experience or hierarchy can stimulate this.

Resistance can be recognised and addressed within the set by the members and a facilitator. An atmosphere of trust in the set ensures psychological safety and builds empathy, but this often takes time to develop.

Linking Learning and Work

For many people joining a set the world of work and that of learning do not seem linked. The former is regarded as an arena of acting and doing, while the latter is concerned with reflecting and theorising. The issue chosen by the set member and sponsor can help to link the two, seemingly distinct, spheres. If the issue is too much like day-to-day work it may not seem like a useful source of learning, but if it is untypical of ordinary work then it may not be seen as relevant so will be more challenging for the set member to see the linkages between work and learning.

Coping Without a Teacher or Trainer

For some set members a typical experience of education and training involves a classroom setting and a teacher, lecturer or trainer. In a set the teacher or trainer does not teach the set members anything and this can be discomforting. It can be addressed by acknowledging such discomfort at the outset, by ensuring equal airtime for everyone and by emphasising the need to cooperate to support the overall learning process. As an example, if set members write down what the facilitator is saying, then this would need to be pointed out as being unnecessary and unhelpful.

Learning from Colleagues

Revans called set members *"comrades in adversity"* and learning from other set members can be enabled, for example, by the notion of needs and offers. At the outset of a set's life (and possibly at intervals thereafter) a facilitator can ask set members to write down what they want and what they have to offer. When shared, this can then lead to person-to-person linkages. It can, however, take time for the process to get going because people can feel selfish in sharing their own hopes and fears and may believe that doing so cannot be illuminating for other set members. Such trust grows over time and requires set members' attention and full engagement.

Reflection

Action learning adds structure to personal experience by providing time and space for reflection. Reflection within the set enables a higher level of awareness of the complexities of the internal (in here) and external (out there) worlds and their inter-connectedness, and this is achieved through support and challenge by set members. Time to reflect in the set encourages set members towards action in the workplace, partly due to peer pressure from their colleagues.

Figure 5.1 Support and challenge.

Support and Challenge

Central to all set meetings are support (or emotional warmth) and challenge. Support cannot be engineered but takes time to build. A sufficient degree of support is needed before any real challenge can be acceptable. Support is derived from active listening and the asking of helpful questions. Asking helpful questions means considering *"Is what I'm about to ask going to be helpful to that person?"* Challenge is to assumptions, perspectives and mindsets. It involves taking the role of devil's advocate and asking, *"What if?"* questions. This is not intended to be aggressive but rather intended to support both reflection and the taking of appropriate action. Too much challenge made too early can be stressful and counterproductive, but too little challenge is also unhelpful. Balancing support and challenge helps the learning process, as shown in Figure 5.1.

Appropriate Behaviour

Appropriate behaviour in sets involves:

- *Concern for the well-being of other set members*: All set members need to care sufficiently about their colleagues to want them to succeed with their issues and to learn from the experience.
- *Empathy*: This is about understanding the role, context and emotional state of other set members. It is not about giving advice, evaluating, making judgements or giving an interpretation.

- ■ *Each set member is an expert on their own issue*: Only by believing that people can help themselves can effective help be given.
- ■ *An action focus*: This means taking those actions agreed in set meetings and reporting back on them.

Leaving a Set

Sometimes a set member will decide to leave a set – possibly due to a change of job, work or home-related problems or a feeling that action learning is not for them. A set member deciding to leave needs to let the set know in advance and advise the set members and facilitator of their reasons.

What Happens in a Set

Set meetings typically move through a series of stages:

- ■ *"What's on top?"*: Set members check-in with each other, noting where they are at and sharing any important news. This helps to reintroduce and reintegrate the set and reconfirm the group's identity, while remaining rooted in workplace realities. A warm-up exercise might be used to assist this, especially early in the set's life.
- ■ *Agenda-setting*: Either the set will confirm what was agreed at the previous meeting or will set an agenda and running order for the current meeting to structure the time available. The principle that all members have equal airtime might be modified by agreement, depending on need or urgency, but this will establish a *"batting order"*. There will be occasions when there are several eager set members and a limited time period and so a limit on how many people can present their issue during a set meeting. There are a variety of ways to address this. They include starting with a *"bidding"* activity where each set member summarises the issue they want to address, together with their enthusiasm or energy level to do so. This can, however, trigger worries about competition or concerns about *being "frozen out"*. Alternatively, the language may be changed to a *"sharing"* round where set members describe their issues without the immediate focus on selection. A further option is to agree *"slots"* in advance, hence avoiding the pressure to choose at the set meeting itself. What is important is that the set members decide on a process that suits the particular dynamics of that set.

- ***Progress-reporting***: Set members take it in turn to describe the current state of play on their issue since the previous meeting. They might give a short presentation and ask for questions and comments. They could ask for questions from other set members to develop a deeper understanding of their issue. They might ask set members to brainstorm, ways of addressing their issue or they might ask the other set members to discuss the issue while they take notes and then review and decide on action.
- ***Action planning***: Agreeing on the next steps which the set member will take in the workplace.
- ***Review***: At the end of each set meeting time is used for reflection, feedback and discussion on the learning process for the set and for individuals. This helps to monitor the effectiveness of the set and ask such questions as:

> *"What worked well today?"*
> *"What was difficult today?"*
> *"Were there any problems with this meeting, and if so, what were they?"*
> *"Do we need to do something different in future?"*
> *"How can we be more effective next time?"*

The set meeting focuses on each set member and their issue in turn, supporting, challenging and questioning, and offering resources such as contacts and source materials. As the set progresses, the balance of time devoted to different activities changes. Time spent on describing the issue and clarifying it declines, while more time is spent on attempting to resolve the issue and the practical actions needed to do this. Similarly, there is a movement from divergent thinking and discussing at an early stage of addressing a set member's issue where there are multiple possibilities and ways forward, towards more convergent thinking and the choice of a next step or steps (5).

Between Set Meetings

To get the most out of set meetings set members need to do some preparation. The most important thing they can do is to take the actions they had agreed at the previous meeting. They can also ask themselves:

> *"What have I done since the last meeting?"*
> *"What are the outstanding actions I previously agreed and why?"*

"Do I still regard the issue as I did earlier?"
"What have I learned so far from what I've done – about myself, others and the issue?"
"Have my plans changed since the last set meeting and why?"
"What do I need from this next set meeting?"
"How can my other set members help me?"

Potential Pitfalls

There are several potential pitfalls regarding successful working in a set. They include:

■ **Some set members have been sent or "volunteered":** These people have not decided themselves to be part of a set so consider that they are there for remedial purposes. It is entirely possible that set membership is not the most appropriate use of their (and the other set members') time. It raises the question as to whether they should continue as a set member.

■ **There is a lack of organisational support:** If the set and the work of the set members are not well-regarded organisationally, this impinges on the credibility of the outcomes of set meetings and on consistency of attendance. Can this be addressed?

■ **Some set members leave it to others to do all the work:** When set members adopt this lack of involvement the issue needs to be addressed openly and early.

■ **Lack of time:** It is better to work effectively on a couple of set members' issues than to cram everyone into a limited time. Time spent at the outset of a set meeting to agree on the use of time is time well-spent.

■ **Losing focus:** This is where set members wander off the point during set meetings and have trouble staying focused. Agreeing an agenda and time slots and checking out with set members whether time is being well-spent will be helpful.

References

1. Vince, R. (2008) "Learning-in-action" and "Learning Inaction": Advancing the Theory and Practice of Critical Action Learning, *Action Learning: Research & Practice*, 5 (2): 93–104

2. Friedman, H. and Booth-Kewley, S. (1987) Personality, Type A Behaviour and Coronary Heart Disease: The Role of Emotional Expression, *Journal of Personality and Social Psychology*, 53 (4): 783–792

3. Gond, J-P, Cabantous, L., Harding, N. and Learmonth, M. (2016) What Do We Mean by Performativity in Organisational and Management Theory? The Uses and Abuses of Performativity, *International Journal of Management Reviews*, 18 (4): 440–463

4. Harrison, R. (1995) Choosing the Depth of Organisational Intervention, in Harrison, R. (Ed.) *The Collected Papers of Roger Harrison*, New York, NY: McGraw-Hill, 13–32

5. Guildford, J. (1967) *The Nature of Human Intelligence*, New York, NY: McGaw-Hill

Chapter 6

Choosing the Issue

"Problem", "project", "topic", "concern", "challenge" and *"question"*. All these words are used, often interchangeably, to characterise the set member's issue that they bring to the set. Many of the problems brought by set members may even be derived from previous *"solutions"*? People may often only have a *"fuzzy"* and general understanding of the area concerned, while alternatively others may feel restricted by the notion of a *"project"*. Whatever term is used, it is the vehicle for action learning so must be demanding without being overwhelming; must address an unresolved issue at some level and may even seem intractable, at least at the outset.

One of the dangers associated with the choice of issue is the *"Einstellung effect"* (1) – that when facing a new problem or challenge, the application is made of a repeated solution learned from previous problems, based upon what is already known, and what people are comfortable with, preventing the discovery of a better way forward.

Revans instead identified what he called the *"risk imperative"* – that the issue chosen should carry some risk of a penalty for failure. Unless set members feel the risk and are aware of what is being risked, then learning is unlikely to happen. If there is no risk, then there is no significant learning.

In considering what issue to tackle, it is important that:

It should be *"live"*: So not be hypothetical. It should be *"here and now"*, not *"there and then"*.

It should matter: It should be real and important to the individual and to the organisation concerned and so not just a contrived issue. So, it should be owned by the set member who can speak from personal experience of the issue. There should be an identified sponsor associated with the issue who will support

 DOI: 10.4324/9781003464440-6

the set member. Key stakeholders should also care about the issue in question. Failure to address the issue would, in time, lead to unfortunate consequences. Ideally, it should be critical and urgent and should trouble and/or excite the set member. Addressing the problem should make a real difference.

It should be practical: It should be based, as far as possible, on quantitative and/or qualitative information and the outcome must have a tangible effect. This means that pursuit of the issue goes beyond diagnosis and into implementation and action. Simply diagnosing an issue without moving towards action has been called *"polishing the problem"*. This may have implications, because the timescale of the set meetings may not always match that of consequential implementation. It should lie within the set member's sphere of influence, or they should be given the requisite authority needed to carry matters to a conclusion.

It should be challenging: It should *"hurt"*, and the status quo should not be an option. It could be something entirely new or something the set member has not previously addressed and which they want to progress.

It should add value: The outcome should benefit both the set member and the organisation.

It should connect: It should build on, or take account of, existing organisational structure, processes and culture, so taking notice of what is realistic and possible.

It should be complex: It should address matters which cross intra-organisational and/or inter-organisational boundaries.

It should be capable of being learned from: So not so specialised that the other set members are unable to challenge and support.

No expert solution should be available: There should be no obvious *"right"* answers and no experts supplying ready-made solutions.

It should not be too large: Too large an issue can be overwhelming and thus frustrating. Significant progress should be possible across the duration of the set. It might be better to only focus initially on one aspect of the issue instead – whatever is most pressing or urgent.

It should be defined in some way: Some issues will be loosely focused, while others will be tightly focused. The former can encourage consideration of different perspectives and allow for ambiguity. The latter may be defined in terms of time and other resources available and the ability and influence of the set member. Whatever the nature of definition, all set members will need to consider:

> *"Whose problem is this?"*
> *"Why is this issue seen as problematic?"*
> *"Is the issue, as presented, symptomatic of something deeper?"*

In fact, the problem is often not the problem, the problem is how we think about the problem (2) because how we think about problems influences how we act on them (3). The issues that set members address can and do come in many shapes and sizes. Revans distinguished between what he called *"puzzles"* and *"problems"*. The former had *"best"* solutions and *"right"* answers. They were *"difficulties from which escapes are thought to be known"* – embarrassments which could be resolved by the application of **P** alone. The latter were complex, rather than complicated; dynamic, rather than static; novel or even recalcitrant. This distinction resembles that between *"tame"* and *"wicked"* problems (4).

Tame Problems (Revans' "Puzzles")

- Can be described by a clear and simple statement.
- Exist where the degree of uncertainty associated with the issue is limited.
- The root causes of the problem are easily known or easily discoverable.
- There is agreement between the interested parties about what *"success"* would look like.
- The issue does not change over the passage of time but remains constant.
- Respond well to planning and management tools and techniques.
- Previous experience and practice with the same or similar issues are guides to a solution.
- Solutions are transferable from one context to another.
- It is understood when a solution has been reached.
- Can be objectively evaluated.

Wicked Problems (Revans' "Problems")

- Are characterised by a high degree of novelty and uncertainty.
- Interact with other issues and cannot be addressed in isolation.
- Appear *"fuzzy"* – incomplete, ambiguous, unclear and even contradictory.
- Demonstrate a lack of relationship between cause and effect.
- Sit across hierarchical, functional, professional and organisational boundaries.
- Seem to defy rational analysis and planning approaches and techniques.
- Have multiple and differing perspectives on what the issue is and what the way forward might be.
- Are strongly related to the particular context in which they are situated.
- Previous experience and practice seem little help towards a resolution.
- Progress will require individuals and organisations to learn new ways of working and to choose between often contradictory values.

- *"Success"* might well be difficult to define, so evaluation will be problematic.
- Resolution of the issue may create further challenging issues.

Many of the latter wicked problems involve tension, contradiction and paradox, all of which are embedded in the everyday. While there is a common individual and organisational tendency towards oversimplification and polarisation, such as addressing wicked problems as if they were tame, it is possible to pursue integration between tensions through *"both/and thinking"* (5).

Action learning can address both tame and wicked problems but is particularly well-suited to working on the latter (6–8). In addressing wicked problems, it is important to understand the paradoxical aspects of the situation. Taking appropriate action may mean letting go and may involve not knowing where you are going, despite having a sense of responsibility. It involves patience, an honest openness and discipline to avoid a *"rush to judgement"*, together with an acceptance of uncertainty and recognition of a feeling of *"lostness"* (9).

It is important to remember that all issues addressed in action learning have a dual public and personal nature. Addressing an issue successfully will involve personal changes as well as external or public changes as problems are reframed at both individual and system levels.

Familiar and Unfamiliar Problems

Figure 6.1 illustrates that problems can be seen as a combination of familiar and unfamiliar tasks and settings. It contains four cells.

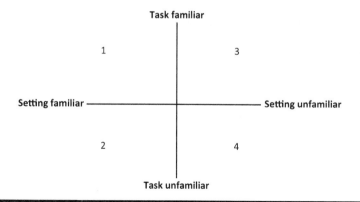

Figure 6.1 Problems familiar and unfamiliar.

Cell 1: Here someone remains in their present job and addresses a familiar issue. The danger is that this may just be a tame issue or puzzle or has been contrived and so does not embody the risk imperative.

Cell 2: Here an individual remains in their current job but tackles an issue they have never previously addressed in that role but is both novel and challenging.

Cell 3: Here someone takes on an issue with which they have previously had some success in their present job but are now faced with the challenge of tackling the same or similar issue in another part of the organisation or in another organisation, and are unfamiliar with the history, culture and ways of working.

Cell 4: Here someone moves to another organisation or an unfamiliar part of their own and tackles an unusual and unfamiliar problem.

While many problems addressed in action learning are in Cells 1 and 2, there is a strong case for Cells 3 and 4 projects which take a set member out of their comfort zone and where they must ask fresh questions and challenge their own long-held assumptions.

Problem-Solving Inputs

There are two major inputs required for action learning to be successful:

Technical (or hard) inputs: These are concerned with task achievement, efficient resource use, attention to detail, the meeting of deadlines, targets and objectives. They emphasise the need to be rational, quantifying and structuring.

Socio-emotional (or soft) inputs: These relate to personal feelings, motivations, and drives. They emphasise the importance of relationships and the need for psychological safety and peer support in the review and reinterpretation of personal experience.

The two inputs are complementary and cannot (and should not) be separated from one another, as Figure 6.2 shows.

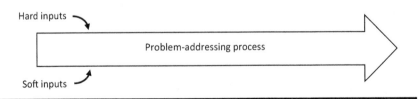

Hard inputs

Problem-addressing process

Soft inputs

Figure 6.2 Inputs to the problem-addressing process.

References

1. Bilalic, M., McLeod, P. and Gobet, F. (2008) Why Good Thoughts Block Better Ones: The Mechanism of the Pernicious Einstellung (Set) Effect, *Cognition*, 108 (3): 652–661
2. Watzlawick, P., Weakland, J. and Fisch, R. (1974) *Change: Principles of Problem Formulation and Problem Resolution*, New York: Norton
3. Crum, A. and Langer, E. (2007) Mindset Matters: Exercise and the Placebo Effect, *Psychological Science*, 18 (2): 165–171
4. Rittel, H. and Webber, M. (1973) Dilemmas in a General Theory of Planning, *Policy Sciences*, 4: 155
5. Smith, W. and Lewis, M. (2022) *Both/And Thinking: Embracing Creative Tensions to Solve Your Toughest Problems*, Boston, MA: Harvard Business School Publishing Corporation
6. Edmonstone, J. (2014) On the Nature of Problems in Action Learning, *Action Learning: Research & Practice*, 11 (1): 25–41
7. Crul, L. (2014) Solving Wicked Problems through Action Learning, *Action Learning: Research & Practice*, 11 (2): 215–224
8. Grint, K. (2008) Wicked Problems and Clumsy Solutions: The Role of Leadership, *Clinical Leaders*, 1 (1): 54–68
9. Von Bulow, C. and Simpson, P. (2022) *Negative Capability in Leadership Practice: Implications for Working in Uncertainty*, London: Palgrave Macmillan

Chapter 7

The Key Skills

There are three major skills associated with working in an action learning set. They are active listening, questioning and giving and receiving feedback. Set members may also be influenced by driver patterns in their behaviour.

Active Listening

Active listening to other set members allows each person to learn about that person's needs and wants so they can understand better what motivates them and what makes them feel valued. This, in turn, serves to enhance empathy and trust. The intention is to enable each set member to express themselves as openly as possible, to be sympathetically heard and understood and to be able to think aloud. There are four elements to active listening:

- *Listening:* This is listening with real attention to try to understand the thoughts and feelings of another person, without wanting to change them in any way. It can focus on a set member's thinking, feelings and intentions (1). Some hints for effective active listening are:
  - Seeing the person as a person and not as a role, label or category.
  - Facing the set member who is talking with an upright and open posture that conveys attention by looking interested and alert. Crossed arms and legs instead convey a closed stance.
  - Maintenance of eye contact.
  - Ensuring minimum distractions such as fidgeting or playing with pens or phones.

 DOI: 10.4324/9781003464440-7

- Attending to more than the set member's words – noting the language used, the tone of voice and the body language.
- Leaving pauses and allowing for silence so the set member can reflect internally and privately. Going along with the words, silence and rhythm of the set member.
- Not leaping in with personal anecdotes about similar experiences but rather listening without interruption, and so taking a cue from the set member before intervening.
- Stopping internal *"self-talk"* and not trying to plan what you intend to say next. Suspending your anxious advocacy and your expectations of what a *"good"* outcome might be.

■ *Paraphrasing back*: This involves using at least some of the set member's words to let them know that they have been heard.

■ *Checking understanding*: Asking the set member whether your perception of what they have said is accurate or not.

■ *Suspending judgment*: Keeping reactions on a leash, so not jumping in to *"fix"* problems – this is both disrespectful and disempowering, and most likely done for your own benefit, rather than theirs.

Active listening can be hampered by:

■ *Comparison*: Making comparisons between oneself and what a set member is saying.

■ *Rehearsing:* Preoccupied with our own response to what the set member is saying.

■ *Second-guessing*: Not allowing the set member to tell their story at their own pace.

■ *Listening with sympathy, not empathy*: Getting in the way of helping a set member to move on.

■ *Inattention:* Distracted by our own emotions or by tiredness.

■ *Evaluative listening*: Imposing our own values on a set member and judging what we hear while it is being communicated.

Questioning

Insightful questioning grows out of active listening. The quality of the questions asked is a function of our ability to listen actively. Questions are used to enable a set member to broaden or deepen their view of their issue and to take responsibility for working it through, rather than being given solutions or ways forward by others. Good questions come from a real interest in a set member's experience and offer them an opportunity to reflect further (2).

There are two models relevant to questioning (3). Model 1 involves asking questions in such a way as to get the other person to agree with your view. It advocates that view in a way that limits others' questioning of it and evaluates the other person's view and attributes caused to it. Model 2 involves actively inquiring into another person's views and the reasoning that supports them. Action learning is rooted in Model 2.

Revans suggested that there were three major questions that a set member needed to consider in relation to their issue. They were:

- ■ **Who knows?** Who has useful information? Who has the facts, ideas, principles, concepts and arguments that determine the dimensions of the issue and are not just official policies, opinions, half-truths or personal views? Who knows about the opportunities and inherent difficulties?
- ■ **Who cares?** Who has the emotional investment and energy to mobilise change? Who is involved and committed to an outcome, rather than just talking about the issue in general terms?
- ■ **Who can?** Who has the power, motivation and influence needed to sponsor, to endorse a change effort and to allocate or re-allocate resources to make change happen? Who can say *"Yes"* and so establish and sustain a momentum for change?

Set members often need assistance in translating the issue they want to address from generalised to specific or from complex to focused. Posing the question for the set member as *"How can I ...?"* can be helpful and other useful questions include:

- ■ **What is it that you do?** What is the nature of your work, role or task?
- ■ **What are you trying to do?** What's driving you? What is your motivation?
- ■ **What's important to you about this issue and why do you care?**
- ■ **What are the dilemmas/opportunities in relation to this issue?**
- ■ **What's stopping you?** What are the blockages or obstructions getting in the way?
- ■ **What are your unique contributions to enable this issue to be tackled effectively?**
- ■ **Who and what can help you?** What resources do you need to identify and mobilise?

A good question is selfless and not asked to highlight the cleverness of the questioner or to generate more information for the questioner, but instead is intended as a way of opening up the set member's own views of their issue. Sometimes a pre-amble before a question can establish rapport and credibility by adding background, context and communicating empathy.

Questions can be both helpful and unhelpful. Helpful questions include:

■ **Clarifying questions**: Such as *"Where would you like to start?"*, *"What's the difference between the way things are now and the way you'd like them to be?"* and *"Who will be affected if you are successful?"*

■ **Checking questions**: Checking what the hearer is hearing is correct. This might include *"What have you already tried?"*, *"What are your options for action here?"* and *"Is this true in every situation?"*

■ **Open questions**: Aimed at stimulating an extended free response and beginning with *"Who?"*, *"What?"*, *"Where?"*, *"Which?"*, *"Why?"*, *"When?"* and *"How?"*.

■ **If questions**: These can open a range of possibilities and bring insights and ideas into awareness. They can shift the dialogue from what-is to what-could-be and could include *"If you were to do this, what would it mean for you?"*, *"If you were to succeed in this what would it make possible?"* and *"If you had a good answer to this, what would it be?"*.

■ **Specification questions**: Aimed at eliciting more detail on the issue such as *"What exactly is the issue?"*, *"What do you want to achieve?"*, *"What's the best possible outcome?"*, *"How would you know if you have achieved it?"*, *"How important is it to you?"*, *"Who are "they?"* and *"Everyone?"*.

■ **Justifying questions**: Providing the opportunity for the set member to further explain their reasons, attitudes or feelings. These might include *"What assumptions are you making here?"*, *"How would you explain that to someone else?"* and *"Could you help me to understand better by putting it another way?"*.

■ **Elaborating questions**: Giving the set member the chance to expand on what they have already described. Examples *are "Can you explain?"*, *"Can you give an example?"*, *"Could you say a bit more about that?"* and *"What exactly happened then?"*.

■ **Personal ownership questions**: Emphasising that the set member has a responsibility for owning the issue and making choices about moving it forward. This could include *"How much does this matter to you?"*, *"Who owns this issue?"*, *"How much energy do you have to tackle this?"*, *"What's preventing you from acting?"*, *"Could your own behaviour be contributing to this situation?"*, *"How brave do you feel?"*, and *"How might you help yourself more?"*.

- ■ *Feelings-related questions*: Aimed at teasing out the emotions linked to the issue. Best posed tentatively these could cover *"How do you feel about that?"*, *"Deep down, what do you really want?"*, *"What excites you the most?"* and *"What worries you the most?"*.
- ■ *Hypothetical questions*: These are suggesting *"What if ... .?"* and *"How about ...?"* and are helpful in offering a new idea or challenging a response.
- ■ *Action-focused questions*: Underlining the necessity for choice and for action in the workplace. These could cover *"What will you do next as a result of this session?"*, *"Where could you get more information on this?"*, *"Who could help?"*, *"Who else do you need to talk to that might have an interest in this?"*, *"What could you start to do differently?"*, *"What are your options for action now?"*, *"When will you start?"*, *"What's the first step for you?"* and *"What are you going to do to look after yourself in this?"*.

By contrast, there are also unhelpful questions, and these include:

- ■ *Closed questions*: Which can only be answered by a *"Yes"* or a *"No"*, curtailing the set member's options for responding. They often being with *"Do you ... ?"*, *"Are you ... ?"* or *"Have you ... ?"*
- ■ *Leading questions*: These put the answer in the set member's mouth and demonstrate that that the questioner knows (or thinks they know) the answer.
- ■ *Multiple questions*: Rolling several questions into one, thus confusing the set member.
- ■ *Long-winded questions*: Likely to be misunderstood.
- ■ *Overly probing questions*: When the set member is not ready to answer, given the level of trust in the set.
- ■ *Poorly timed questions*: At an inappropriate point interrupting the set member from working on their issue.
- ■ *Trick questions*: Likely to cause resentment, demotivation and possibly withdrawal.
- ■ *Too many questions*: Feeling like an interrogation and likely to lead to defensiveness.
- ■ *A suggestion disguised as a question:*

It has been suggested (4) that there are three successful stages helping to create a movement from possibilities to decisions to committed action. These are:

- ■ *Could do*: This raises possibilities and options.
- ■ *Want to*: This relates to energy and motivation.
- ■ *Will do*: This is concerned with determination and traction.

There are potential areas to address in this area:

- **Insurance:** This involves helping a set member to identify and focus on the critical factors that could ensure or undermine their success. Helpful questions include:
  - *"Are there any obstacles to getting this done?"*
  - *"Who else do you need to check in with?"*
  - *"On a scale of 1–10, how confident are you that you will complete this step by the deadline?"*
  - *"What would it take to raise that to a 7, 8 or 9?"*
  - *"How could you change the step or the deadline to make this more realistic?"*
  - *"What could you do to increase your chances of getting this done successfully?"*
  - *"Do you need a person or mechanism to help you to do this?"*
- **Equivocation:** If a set member seems to be ambivalent or only superficially committed to a course of action, it is finally the set member's choice as to whether or not they follow through. Helpful questions include:
  - *"Are you really ready to commit to that next step?"*
  - *"What is holding you back from taking that next step?"*
  - *"You said you should do this, but what would make it something that you will do because you really want to do it?"*
  - *"You seem to be procrastinating. You can either do this or not. What will you do?"*

Giving and Getting Feedback

In action learning sets it is inevitable that set members will give and get feedback on their behaviour in the set and, by implication, also on their behaviour in a work setting. Feedback can help set members to understand better the impact of their behaviour and, where necessary, refine it. Feedback says as much about the person giving it as the one receiving it, so it is useful to see it as a conversation to understand the impact of behaviour and the possibility of changing it. It is a focused activity and not to be confused with criticism or praise. It is specific, descriptive and clear, rather than general, personal, judgemental and blaming. So good feedback should be:

- **Owned**: By the person giving it and couched in *"You – I"* statements, such as *"When you … I felt … "*. A description of someone's behaviour should be followed by a statement about the impact of that behaviour such as *"When you banged your fist on the table it made me feel anxious".*

- **Descriptive, not evaluative**: Offered only on specific observable behaviour – clear descriptions of words said or actions taken, rather than supposed personality or mental states. The focus is on what someone does, rather than on the person. It means acting as a mirror and not as a judge. It implies the use of adverbs (referring to actions) rather than adjectives (referring to qualities), so it frequently begins with *"When you did ..."* or *"When you said ..."*

- **Directed**: It should be focused on behaviour that a set member can do something about, emphasising what might be done differently.

- **Balanced**: It should consider the needs of the receiver as well as those of the giver.

- **Well-timed:** Feedback should be provided as close to the situation that is being described as possible, rather than saved to be delivered later, but obviously it also depends upon a set member's readiness to hear it.

- **Specific, not general or abstract**: It is important to avoid evaluating, making generalisations or using abstractions. It is more meaningful if reference is made to the here-and-now, rather than to the there-and-then or the time-to-time.

- **Solicited**: Feedback is better if it is asked for rather than imposed.

- **Communicated clearly**: Thinking about what to say and how to say it in advance of saying it is helpful.

- **In appropriate amounts**: Not stored up but delivered in *"digestible"* amounts.

Receiving feedback can be challenging, but good rules of thumb are:

- **Say thank you**
- **Listen carefully before responding**: A kneejerk reaction could be to respond immediately but listening (although possibly uncomfortable) can provide insights which otherwise might be missed.
- **Be clear about what is being said**: Check out what is being heard before responding to it.
- **Decide on what action to take**: The choices could be to ignore the feedback or to accept it and use it as a basis for changed future action.

Driver Patterns

Set members are likely to have personal driver patterns concerned with the way they think about or respond to different situations and challenges (5). Assessing these driver patterns can help to identify causes of success and non-success and to learn from them. The driver patterns are based on the powerful myth that behaving in a specific manner will make things better. They are a myth because they contain partial truths – powerfully positive when used in proportion, but negative when over-used. Some of the typical driver patterns are:

- ■ *Be strong:* The benefits of this pattern are:
  - Being calm under pressure.
  - Taking unpleasant decisions.
  - Being reliable and conscientious.
  - Being even-tempered.

- ■ The drawbacks or costs of this pattern are:
  - Being seen as cold and unemotional
  - Getting overloaded.
  - Being perceived as unsupportive of others.
  - Hating admitting to personal weaknesses.

- ■ *Be perfect:* As benefits we can be seen as:
  - Someone who takes responsibility.
  - Someone who is well-organised.
  - A person who prepares thoroughly.
  - A produced of reliable and accurate work.
  - Someone who makes contingency plans.

- ■ But the drawbacks are:
  - Work we deliver may well be late.
  - We may get lost in the detail and lose the bigger picture.
  - We may have difficulty in delegating to others.
  - We may become overly self-critical.

- ■ *Please other people:* This can produce benefits such as:
  - Being seen as a good team member.
  - Showing genuine interest in others.
  - Being intuitive and empathetic.
  - Helping others resolve conflict.

The drawbacks, however, are:

- ■ Being indecisive and unassertive regarding own needs.
- ■ Avoiding criticism or taking things personally.
- ■ Avoiding conflictful situations.

- Try hard: The benefits are that we gain a reputation for:
  - Being enthusiastic.
  - Showing initiative and creativity.
  - Linking new things.
  - Indicating high motivation.
  - Volunteering to do things.

- But the drawbacks include:
  - Appearing poor at finishing things.
  - Missing deadlines.
  - Appearing to have too broad a focus.
  - Appearing to have disorganised communication.

- *Hurry up*: The benefits can be to be known as someone who:
  - Works quickly.
  - Gets a lot done.
  - Enjoys challenges.
  - Uses time effectively.
  - Operates well under pressure.

The drawbacks are that a person can be seen as:

- Impatient.
- Delaying what they see as non-urgent tasks.
- Someone who has instrumental relationships, just as a means to an end.
- Poor at planning work out in advance.

Likewise, set members can feel *"stuck"* because their driver pattern or mindset (6) tells them that:

- There are *"right"* answers, so they must find that answer.
- Imagination is soft and fluffy, and they are a hard-thinking serious person.
- They need to follow the rules.
- They are practical, and don't explore or even dream.
- Being playful is frivolous – you cannot have fun and be successful.
- This is not my area, so I'm not interested in unusual connections.
- I don't like ambiguity.

Action learning can help people to examine their driver patterns and challenge the *"stuckness"*.

Non-Verbal Approaches

To free up dialogue with and between set members there is a case for using non-verbal and visual approaches. These include:

- *Postcards*: A series of postcards with a variety of scenes and things may be laid out and set members are invited to choose a card or cards to express a view or tell a story, which they must be willing to tell the other set members. This uses visual cues to open up different types of insight.
- *Object sculpting*: Set members are invited to bring objects from work or home and place them as they choose. The placement of the objects and the relationships between them can reveal symbolic meanings (7).
- *Rich pictures*: This involves set members drawing a situation that illustrates the main elements and relationships that need to be considered in seeking to understand it and make an improvement. It consists of pictures, text, symbols and icons used to illustrate the situation graphically. Rich pictures visualise the complex systems nature of a situation, open up discussion, generate creativity and insight and facilitate shared understanding (8).

References

1. Cole, M. and Higgins, J. (2023) *The Great Unheard at Work: Understanding Voice and Silence in Organisations*, Abingdon: Routledge
2. Marquardt, M. and Tiede, B. (2023) *Leading with Questions: How Leaders Discover Powerful Answers by Knowing How and What to Ask*, Hoboken, NJ: John Wiley
3. Argyris, C. (1993) *Knowledge for Action: A Guide to Overcoming Barriers to Organisational Change*, San Francisco, CA: Jossey-Bass
4. Stoltzfus, T. (2008) *Coaching Questions: A Coach's Guide to Powerful Asking Skills*, Redding CA: Coach22 Bookstore LLC
5. Edmonstone, J. (2013) *Personal Resilience for Healthcare Staff: When the Going Gets Tough*, London: Radcliffe Publishing
6. Chivers, M. and Pedler, M. (2010) *DIY Handbook for Action Learning*, Prescot: Mersey Care NHS Trust
7. Heinl, P. (1988) Object Sculpting, Symbolic Communication and Early Experience: A Single Case Study, *Journal of Family Therapy*, 10: 167–178
8. Williams, B. and Hummelbrunner, R. (2010) *Systems Concepts in Action: A Practitioner's Toolkit*, Sanford, CA: Sanford University Press

Chapter 8

The Energy Investment Model

Set members bring to the set a combination of energy and attitude which produces identifiable styles of behaviour, rather than types of people. Everyone has different energy levels and states of mind at different times and, as a result, our behaviour always has an impact on others. Everyone gets the most from an experience when their personal energy is high and their attitude is positive, but if this is not achievable for individuals it can create difficulties for the set membership.

Figure 8.1 shows two dimensions – *energy*, which can be high or low, and *attitude*, which can be positive or negative. This creates four cells in the matrix – Spectator, Victim, Cynic and Player.

Spectators: Spectators have a positive attitude but low energy and tend to feel:

- Positive about what is happening and want to contribute.
- Anxious and lacking in confidence.
- Reluctant to get involved in the work of the set.
- Threatened when too exposed by the set's working.
- Reluctant to take risks.
- More comfortable when watching on the sidelines.

They tend to react by:

- Acknowledging the good ideas of others but being reluctant to change themselves.

DOI: 10.4324/9781003464440-8

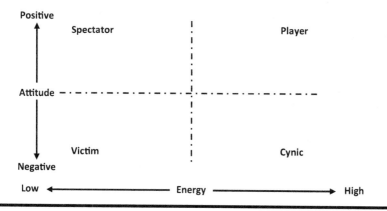

Figure 8.1   Energy investment model.

- Working harder than ever at their own previously successful behaviour.
- Avoiding taking undue risks.
- Trying to ride things out until things return to normal.
- Keeping a low profile.

The kind of support that Spectators need includes:

- Understanding and help in coping with their fear and lack of confidence.
- Effective role models.
- Plenty of feedback, encouragement and positive reinforcement from other set members.
- Stretching but achievable challenges, both in terms of the issue and in relation to their behaviour vis-à-vis other set members.

The kind of questions which will stimulate Spectators are:

- *"Why do you think this might not apply to you?"*
- *"Who will do this for you if you don't do it for yourself?"*
- *"How could you justify leaving this to others?"*
- *"What's stopping you from having a go?"*
- *"Can you afford to miss this opportunity?"*

Victims: Victims have a negative attitude and low energy. They tend to have bruised self-esteem and feel:

- Unhappy or depressed.

- Overwhelmed by work.
- Powerless and fearful of mistakes.

They tend to react in set meetings and at work by:

- Blocking-out challenges.
- Avoiding confronting issues.
- Retreating into safety.
- Avoiding risk and doing the minimum necessary.
- Avoiding thinking about what might happen.

The support that Victim set members need includes:

- Understanding and help in dealing with their stress and frustration.
- Peer encouragement.
- A series of small challenges and successes to rebuild their confidence.

Useful questions for Victim set members include:

- *"Do you really want to feel like this?"*
- *"How much can you get back in control?"*
- *"Who might help you to do this?"*
- *"What could you do to make a start?"*
- *"What's the worst thing that could possibly happen if you tried something new?"*

Cynics: Cynic set members have high energy but a negative attitude and tend to feel:

- Not listened to at work (and so also potentially by fellow set members) and thus excluded and constrained.
- Rebellious and determined to block any change they do not personally own.
- Surprised at the stress felt by others.
- That they are *"right"* – and angry at the world for ignoring them.
- Frustrated by what they see as other people's confusing and whinging.
- Overly confident in their own ability.

They tend to react by:

- Expressing their frustration over the discomfort and hesitancy displayed by others.

- Arguing against changes and always seeing the negative.
- Pressing for quick solutions and decisive actions – and then criticising them!
- Being oblivious to the consequences of their negativity on others.
- Bringing both Victims and Spectators round to their perspective.

The support which they need includes:

- Humouring – but only to a point.
- To be given a chance to take personal responsibility for their actions.
- Pairing with a Player set member.
- Being confronted about the negative aspects of their behaviour.
- Being reminded about what the set and the issue are for.
- Clear ground rules and boundaries.

Helpful questions for Cynic set members include:

- *"How much do you know about the impact you have on others?"*
- *"What happened to make you feel this way?"*
- *"Could you see things differently?"*
- *"Could you get a better return on your efforts? How might you do that?"*
- *"Would there be a better time to do this?"*

Players: Players have a positive attitude and high energy, so make excellent set members. They typically feel:

- Challenged and stretched by both their issue and by interaction with other set members.
- Comfortable with the need to change.
- Open to possibilities and ideas and to contributions made by other set members.
- Optimistic about the future.
- Feeling in control of their own destiny.
- Not afraid of short-term mistakes and setbacks.

They tend to react by:

- Seeking the longer-term silver lining behind the short-term dark clouds.
- Viewing ambiguity and change as challenge and opportunity.
- Finding humour in different situations and using it in their interactions with others.

- Treating life (not just their job, issue and the set) as a continual learning experience.
- Expanding their personal comfort zone.

Player set members need:

- Reward and support from their peers for being key to change and transition.
- Flexible personal development opportunities coupled with tangible and visible rewards.
- Latitude to do things their way and model this effective behaviour to others.
- Support from others when they take a stand against a Cynic set member.
- Respect, recognition and thanks from colleagues in the set.
- Not to have all the work of the set dumped on them.

Useful questions for Player set members include:

- *"Are you taking others along with you or are you too far ahead of the pack?"*
- *"Might others see you as chameleon-like, or as flip and shallow?"*
- *"How sensitive are you to the fear of change in others?"*
- *"Is your optimism regarding the future well-founded or not?"*

The energy investment model can serve as a means of identifying exactly where set members appear to be and what might be needed to move matters forward.

(An earlier version of this chapter appeared as "Learning and Development in Action Learning: The Energy Investment Model", Industrial and Commercial Training 35 (1): 2003: 26–28.)

Chapter 9

Dealing with Anxiety

Anxiety is the distress or uneasiness caused by fear of danger or misfortune. It may be real or imagined, currently present or vague and anticipated emotionally or psychologically. If a person experiences too little anxiety there will be no motivation to change. Too much anxiety can have destructive or self-limiting effects which means that people may deny, deflect, distort, defend or be fearful of change. They will be wary in trusting others and be likely to avoid experimentation. Only when there is enough anxiety to motivate a search for new thoughts and behaviours, but not so much as to lead to fearful debilitation, can anxiety enable change and provide the energy needed to risk being honest, direct, challenging and different (1).

It is worth remembering that many (if not most) organisations are built on the bureaucratic principle that rationality should govern at the expense of emotions (2). What takes place in an action learning set is not just a rational or intellectual process but is also an emotional one because each set member has, in the past, experienced both positive and negative life and work situations which they view through the template of their emotional and psychological history. These experiences will have been shaped through membership of family, work, professional, organisational and social groupings and by broader economic, social and political forces. As a result, many people deploy a range of emotional and perceptual filters as a means of anxiety reduction, including denial, avoidance and oversimplification.

Because action learning involves the risk of failure it inevitably involves anxiety. Anxiety is an integral aspect of set membership and contributes to the success and failure of sets. Anxiety may stem from a set member's work role, career situation, the nature of the issue they bring to the set and the purpose and

DOI: 10.4324/9781003464440-9

nature of the set itself. For example, set members may not understand exactly what is happening in a set meeting while they are trying to make sense of it all. They will be concerned over whether they will be accepted or rejected by their fellow members and whether they are *"doing it right"* (3). Since action learning is open-ended, emergent and therefore unpredictable anxiety is most probably endemic. This is quite different from conventional education and training approaches where uncertainty is constrained, and order is seemingly established through curricula and adherence to *"best"* practices. Anxiety can therefore get in the way of risk and experimentation by set members and typical examples of anxiety-induced behaviour include:

- *A reluctance to join in*: Unwillingness to be creative with behaviour and ideas. Not asking *"What if ... ?"* questions resulting in seemingly overly serious behaviour.
- *A narrow self-view*: Low self-assessment of personal abilities and resources and an inability or unwillingness to recognise the personal contribution that could be made to help other set members.
- *Fear of losing face*: Worried about being seen as admitting incompetence or of having backed down.
- *Fear of recrimination*: Concern that changing personal behaviour might make other set members or work colleagues angry and resentful.
- *Fear of losing control*: And so, ending up in a bigger mess than it is perceived already exists.
- *Fear of failure*: In the eyes of other set members and/or of work colleagues, leading to an unwillingness to take even calculated risks; an undervaluing of the importance of feelings and a lack of spontaneity in interaction with others.
- *Fear of ambiguity*: Avoidance of matters lacking clarity or where outcomes are unknown or unpredictable. Reluctance to try things out and an overemphasis on the known at the expense of the unknown.
- *Fear of disorder*: A dislike of complexity and a preference for order and structure, usually expressed in terms of opposites such as good versus bad, or right versus wrong.
- *Fear of looking foolish*: Attracting negative comments about seeming to act out of character.
- *Fear of being vulnerable*: Not knowing what might happen by trying a different approach.
- *Fear of letting someone else make a mistake*: Feeling responsible for the decisions and actions of others.
- *Fear of influencing others*: Not wanting to appear aggressive, hence hesitation in identifying with emerging points of view.

The source of anxiety may be the set member's current work role, problems in their organisational setting, the chosen issue, the purpose and nature of the set itself and their place within it. This may lead to the development of defensive routines (4) – unconscious strategies for self-protection which limit the potential to learn. These will have been acquired over time and through experience because it is believed that they can keep us safe but really keep us in stuck behaviour patterns. They could include:

- Using the set as a kind of ***therapy group*** to explore personal issues at the expense of addressing work-related problems.
- Set members acting as a ***collective agony aunt*** in an advice-giving mode, with little attempt to listen actively to what a set member is saying – and avoiding saying.
- Using the set as a *"vicar's tea-party"* or ***pleasant social gathering*** – a holiday from the rigours of organisational life.
- Set members portraying themselves to other set members as ***heroes*** (self-idealising) or ***villains*** (self-deprecating).

Confronting anxiety may involve set members relinquishing their previous work roles, ideas and practices to create, find or discover new and more adaptable ideas, ways of thinking and acting, and so deal with the instability of changing conditions and the insecurity which such change provokes. This is the process of *"unlearning"* whereby well-established patterns of thinking and behaving are interrupted and breached and redundant mindsets are re-evaluated, re-positioned and embodied in a wider repertoire of possible responses. It is not about forgetting but with advancing by slowing down, stepping back and letting go from prior understanding that may limit the future (5,6).

Anxiety can have destructive or self-limiting effects but can also provide the energy needed to be honest, direct and challenging. Confronting anxiety may require set members to relinquish earlier roles, ideas and practices to discover or create new ways of thinking and acting.

One way of dealing with anxiety is to seek sanctuary in the views of experts who seem to produce anxiety-reducing answers and so offer what seems like safety and security. Action learning focuses on helping people to own their issues – with all the messiness, confusion and uncertainty which that entails, rather than relying on expert advice. It provides the necessary time and space needed for people to express their worries, hopes and fears and to reflect, review, develop understanding and plan for the future. The minimal structure provided by the ground rules offers a useful means of containing set members' anxiety, as shown in Figure 9.1.

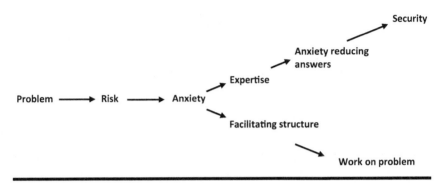

Figure 9.1 Alternative means of dealing with anxiety.

The set provides a holding and enabling framework in which set members' anxieties can be faced, comprehended and worked through with the appropriate balance of support and challenge. This helps to develop *"negative capability"*, a term coined by the poet John Keats, which he described as a state in which a person *"is capable of being in uncertainties, mysteries, doubts without any irritable reaching after facts and reason"* (7). It is the capacity to live with and tolerate ambiguity and paradox, to remain content with half-knowledge and to accommodate change in a non-defensive manner, without being overwhelmed by the ever-present pressure to react (8).

So, it is important to acknowledge that anxiety is likely to be present in a set, to admit that this is the case and that it is legitimate to express it and to recognise that doing so can help to address the contradiction and paradox in personal and organisational life (9). Action learning can enable anxiety to be acknowledged, reflected on and worked with, rather than dismissed or repressed (10). Learning in this way can clearly involve vulnerability and risk-taking as people admit to the limits of their understanding or even to a lack of understanding, but the set offers a haven of psychological safety so that set members are able to manage their anxiety in such a way that enables courageous and creative thinking and action without minimising the nature and scale of the challenges faced (11). As they do so, there may be *"failures"*, but it is possible to learn as much from failing as from succeeding. As the playwright Samuel Beckett said *"Ever tried. Ever failed. No matter. Try again. Fail again, Fail better"* (12). The action in action learning is there as the pathway to learning. While solving a problem or issue is good, it is not ultimately critical that there be problem resolution, as much as there be learning from the experience. It is preferable to fail at finding a solution to a problem yet obtain learning than to fail to learn while obtaining a solution to a problem (13).

References

1. Marshak, R. (2016) Anxiety and Change in Contemporary Organisation Development, *OD Practitioner*, 48 (1): 11–19
2. Goleman, D. (1996) *Emotional Intelligence: Why It Can Matter More Than IQ*, New York, NY: Bantam Books
3. Pedler, M. and Abbott, C. (2008) Am I Doing It Right? Facilitating Action Learning for Service Improvement, *Leadership in Health Services*, 21 (3): 185–199
4. Argyris, C. (1985) *Strategy, Change and Defensive Routines*, London: Pitman Publishing
5. Brook, C., Pedler, M., Abbott, C. and Burgoyne, J. (2016) On Stopping Doing Those Things That Are Not Getting Us to Where We Want to Be: Unlearning and Critical Action Learning, *Human Relations*, 69 (2): 369–389
6. Chokr, N. (2009) *Unlearning or How Not to Be Governed*, Exeter: Societas Imprint Academic
7. Keats, J. (1899) *The Complete Poetical Works and Letters of John Keats*, Cambridge: Houghton Mifflin
8. Hirsch, C., von Bulow, C. and Simpson, P. (2023) Stoicism, Philosophy as a Way of Life, and Negative Capability: Developing a Capacity for Working in Radical Uncertainty, *Leadership (Forthcoming)*
9. Von Bulow, C. and Simpson, P. (2022) *Negative Capability in Leadership Practice: Implications for Working in Uncertainty*, London: Palgrave Macmillan
10. Pedler, M. and Abbott, C. (2013) *Facilitating Action Learning: A Practitioner's Guide*, Maidenhead: Open University Press/McGraw-Hill
11. Linklater, J. and Kellner, K. (2008) Don't Just Do Something – Stand There: Using Action Learning to Help Organisations Work with Anxiety, *Action Learning: Research and Practice*, 5 (2): 167–172
12. Beckett, S. (1995) *Nohow On*, London: Grove Press
13. Raelin, J. (2000) *Work-Based Learning: The New Frontier of Management Development*, Upper Saddle, NJ: Prentice-Hall

Chapter 10

Supporting, Recording, Ending

A wide range of potential support material and activities exist that can form part of the action learning process. Some of these are contained in Chapter 15. All such material should be used with care and discrimination because there is a danger of confusing means with ends. Such support material can, however, be helpful because of the overwhelming seductiveness of the issue being addressed by a set member, possibly leading them to be obsessed with action achievement alone, at the expense of learning. Support material can therefore be useful in diverting people away from task obsession and towards consideration about the processes by which tasks are achieved. Good support material can force explicit discussion within the set of both the *"in here"* (intra-set) and *"out there"* (workplace) learning processes and achievements.

Support material should be used when:

- It has been presented and described to the set members.
- They have had sufficient time and opportunity to consider the advantages and disadvantages of using it.
- They make a conscious decision to use the material.

Diagnostics

Questionnaire-based diagnostics can help set members assess their personal styles and preferences. Among those which have been used are the Myers-Briggs

DOI: 10.4324/9781003464440-10

Type Instrument (MBTI), the Thomas Kilmann Conflict Mode Instrument, the Belbin Team Roles Questionnaire and the Career Orientations Inventory. Other diagnostics focus on individual learning styles and the self-diagnostic Learning Styles Inventory developed by David Kolb (1) was a forerunner but has been criticised as embodying a rationalistic approach and as being culture-bound, so has found less favour as time has passed. The Learning Styles Questionnaire (LSQ) devised by Peter Honey and Alan Mumford (2) has proved more popular. It identifies four learning styles:

- *Activist:* Someone who likes to take direct action and thrives on learning from challenges and new experiences. Activists are enthusiastic and welcome new challenges but are less interested in what happened in the past or in putting matters into a broader context. They are interested in the here-and-now, like to have a go, try things out and participate.
- *Reflector:* Someone who likes to think about things in detail before acting, so more cautious, standing back and examining experiences from different angles. They take a thoughtful approach, are good listeners and prefer to adopt a low profile.
- *Theorist:* Someone who likes to see how things fit into an overall pattern. They are logical and objective systems people who prefer a sequential approach to problems. They are analytical, pay much attention to detail and adapt and integrate their observations into sound theories.
- *Pragmatist:* Someone who likes to see how things work out in practice. They are practical and down-to-earth preferring to solve problems, try out new ideas and techniques to see whether they work in practice.

While each person develops their own profile across these styles an individual's learning style is not something which is fixed and is capable of change, especially in response to different external situations and influences, such as a change in work setting. Information derived from the LSQ should never be used to avoid types of learning but should provide a basis for developing a more balanced learning approach.

An action learning set is more valuable where individuals from different learning styles are represented in the set membership, and less useful when the set members all have the same or similar learning style. People with different learning styles derived from different areas of experience make the best set members because their line of thought and action provokes the most challenging and enlightening questions from other set members.

There are also dangers in using the LSQ as a typology – a means of dividing people into discreet categories. When people pin labels on themselves they may believe that, once they have identified their predominant learning styles, it is a fixed trait which cannot be changed, so they must work within that limitation, seeking only those experiences matching their preferred style and avoiding those offering a potentially different approach. Thus, learners potentially develop self-limiting implicit beliefs about themselves that could become self-fulfilling prophecies. Nevertheless, a survey of UK academics found that some 58% of them accepted using diagnostics such as the LSQ as being effective (3). Used with care, the LSQ can support action learning, with the rider that it should never be mistaken for an end, but only as a means to an end – the stimulation of the learning process.

Learning Diaries

Learning diaries have two purposes. One is to record a set member's experience across the duration of the set meetings and the other is to make linkages between what happens in the set and what happens in the workplace, to develop reflection on experience. Set members need to be completely frank and sincere in what they write and exercise a degree of self-discipline in finding the time and space to update the diary regularly. The reflective process can be aided by including such things as quotable quotes, cartoons and journal clippings.

A learning diary needs to be both sequential and reflective.

- ■ **Sequential**: This involves jotting down notes on a continuing and regular basis under such headings as:
  - **People**: The behaviour of people in the set and/or the workplace who make an important impact on the set member.
  - **Events**: Key incidents that take place at work or in the set meeting.
  - **Reactions**: How the set member thought and felt and what they did.
- ■ **Reflective**: This involves consideration of:
  - **Insights**: Ideas or thoughts that made a significant impact on the set member – either their own contributions or those of other set members.
  - **Learning**: What sense is being made of what is happening to themselves and others in both the set and the workplace. This can be stimulated by such questions as:

    "When did I feel most engaged and why?"
    "When did I feel most distanced and why?"
    "When did I feel most puzzled and why?"
    "When did I feel most affirmed and why?"
    "What gaps in my learning did I discover and how should I go about filling them?"

In this way, a learning diary should be both ***retrospective*** (looking back to understand what has happened) and ***prospective*** (looking forward and deciding what to do next).

Recording

What happens in a set meeting is not what happens in a formal and structured meeting of committees, project teams, task forces and working groups where minutes capture the issues covered, the discussion that took place and the decisions that were made. However, there is real value in keeping a record of what goes on in a set meeting and this can take the form of notes, mind maps, pictures, symbols, metaphors or quotations which capture important learning points. There is merit in asking at each set meeting for one person to be responsible for taking brief notes and then circulating these, especially for agreed actions or requests for information or resources.

Ending

Almost all sets run for an agreed and finite time but there is often a desire on the part of set members for the set to continue after it is officially over. This may be because, for many set members, the combination of support and challenge which they experience is unique in relation to the remainder of their work or life experience. Action learning sets are not permanent entities, so the question of the self-life of sets is important.

Given the level of commitment required from set members, each set will need to review regularly whether it continues to meet the needs of set members and there will come a time when that configuration of people and issues is no longer effective. Sets which continue to meet, either out of habit or because it is comfortable to do so will not really be productive – and this will quickly become obvious.

Ending the life of a set should not be seen as a failure because a good test of action learning is if the set knows when it is right to stop, rather than continuing in a sterile manner. If a set has worked well, it should be mature enough to realise that as much has been achieved as can be achieved and so the time has come to stop. The ending of the set is thus part of the development process itself – a symbol of growth, rather than loss.

The final set session might include the following:

■ Set members recapturing the way they felt when first coming to the set.

- Reflecting on the original aims of the set, discovering what each set member has achieved and so reminding of how far each set member has come.
- Sharing how they are feeling at the end of a set's life.

Some sets may continue to meet socially while others may continue virtually. The processes which set members have gone through and the relationships which they have built, fostered and maintained will prove valuable to them after the set has ended and in a variety of other settings. Lessons learned by set members will continue to resonate long after the set has gone.

Some self-managing sets may continue for years where set members continue to derive benefit from such involvement. The benefits from such long-term sets include the fostering of a sense of community and trust, continual personal and professional development of the set members and a context which is both whole-life and lifelong. The downside is that the cohesiveness of the set can be challenging to any potential new members and that anyone leaving the set will undoubtedly have a significant impact (4).

References

1. Kolb, D. (1984) *Experiential Learning*, Englewood Cliffs, NJ: Prentice-Hall
2. Honey P. and Mumford, A. (1995) *Using Your Learning Styles*, 2nd edition, Maidenhead: Peter Honey Publications
3. Newton, P. and Miah, M. (2017) Evidence-Based Higher Education: Is the Learning Styles "Myth" Important? *Frontiers in Psychology*, 8 (444): 211–221
4. Yates, C. (2023) Twenty-Five Years: A Self-Managed Action Learning Set, *Action Learning: Research & Practice*, 20 (1): 60–66

Chapter 11

The Facilitator Role

Revans was sceptical about even the necessity for action learning sets to have permanent facilitators. Insofar as one was ever necessary, it was to act as a kind of *"mirror"* to illustrate the conditions in the set, such that the set members could learn by themselves and from each other. Despite this, most action learning sets do begin life with a named facilitator (sometimes variously called a set adviser, coach, team coach, host or learning lead), who is there to aid the overall learning process by helping to create and sustain the conditions which make it possible for set members to learn from their own experience and from their fellow set members. The facilitator is therefore not a set leader, convenor or chair but is the *"guide on the side"* rather than the *"sage on the stage"* (1). So, the role is not to teach, act as an expert consultant, manage the set or report what occurs in the set to others, but to enable the learning and action which are the focus of the set's existence. While the facilitator typically does have initial responsibility for the *"governance"* aspects of a set's functioning (the establishment and adherence to ground rules and agreed processes) the key emphasis is not one of control, but rather of curiosity, respect and support.

Facilitators can be *"internals"* or *"externals"*. Internal facilitators are employed by an organisation and will most likely know it very well, so will probably have insight and understanding on the need for action learning. They may be able to see beyond the *"presenting"* issues and may have established a good reputation and track record. However, they may also be part of the culture that needs to change and may have been *"pointed at"* problems and people by senior leaders. The perceived status of the internal facilitator may therefore be either valued or not. External action learning facilitators also come with certain advantages and disadvantages. They may have a well-established reputation and

DOI: 10.4324/9781003464440-11

appear to be independent, neutral and objective vis-à-vis their client organisation. However, they may have little or no understanding about the internal organisational culture, history and micro-politics.

Any facilitator is most active early in the set's life, being involved in setting it up, helping set members to find their feet, getting to know each other and seeking agreement on ground rules. All this activity is intended to *"jump-start"* the set. Henceforward, the facilitator's intentions are limited to where and when help can be given, so they need to be judicious, tentative, gentle and timely, based on the overall intention of being helpful and fostering learning.

As a set proceeds the facilitator role moves from energising and speeding matters up to slowing things down and encouraging reflection and for enabling set members to take responsibility for their actions. As they do so energy levels in sets can vary from set members being *"fired-up"* to *"wilting"* and the facilitator needs to be alert to such mood changes, to draw set members' attention to them and ask for suggestions for addressing this. Chapter 8 offers one model for identifying the state-of-play for individual set members. Some activities which can develop a sense of stamina in a set include:

- Sharing telephone numbers and/or email addresses to encourage contact between set meetings.
- Encouraging meetings of pairs and trios between agreed set meetings, either face-to-face or virtually.
- Encouraging informal lunchtime meetings.

Qualities Required of Facilitators

These include:

- *An overwhelming desire to help people learn*: Set members' learning is likely to happen slowly, personally and often privately. So, the facilitator will often have to *"bite their tongue"* and not intervene to allow this process to occur. At other times the facilitator will actively encourage the involvement of quieter or withdrawn set members.
- *Patience*: Set members will work and learn at quite different speeds, both within the set meetings and in their work setting, so their skills of insight and inquiry may well take time to evolve.
- *Empathy*: An ability to stand in another's shoes and to see the world through their eyes.
- *Tolerance of ambiguity*: A facilitator operates in a realm of uncertainty and needs to let set members take control where this is appropriate.

- *Openness and frankness*: Recognising and expressing personal feelings in set meetings, provided they contribute to the overall learning process.
- *Self-doubt*: The ability to admit personal uncertainties in a way that does not threaten the set's security but rather reveals the facilitator's humanity.
- *Proportion*: An ability to summarise and see the *"big picture"*, make sense of what is happening and demonstrate an awareness of the broader context for set members.
- *Micro-politics*: An understanding of the local dynamics within the organisation or organisations concerned regarding how things get done, where power and influence lie and how they might be mobilised.
- *Role model*: Modelling the behaviour that s/he espouses so there is a match between what is said and what is done.

Some have also suggested that a track record of experience in the employment field concerned can be helpful so that a *"bilingual ability"* can be demonstrated, showing familiarity with the wider organisational system, identifying repeated behaviour patterns, blockages and dysfunctions (2), although this could also potentially be seductive and lead the facilitator into the temptation of adopting an expert role.

These comments relate largely to mainstream action learning. In Critical Action Learning (CAL) especially the facilitator has a key role in helping to engage with the underlying emotions and power relationships that are inevitably embedded in sets, and that both promote and prevent learning and, as a result, the facilitator role is a much more pro-active one (3).

Facilitator Skills

In mainstream action learning the skills which the facilitator needs to demonstrate are:

- *Choosing the issues that help*: Out of everything that is going on in the set the facilitator tracks and chooses those issues that link this to the parallel challenges described by set members in their work settings.
- *Asking good questions*: Questions which make set members both think and feel, but also feel supported and challenged as they find their own solutions to their issues. There will also be occasions when the best question is silence.
- *An understanding of group processes:* Especially the difference between task and process and between helpful and unhelpful behaviour.
- *Choosing the right language*: Being aware of the dangers of jargon, abbreviations, intellectualising, talking down and mystification.

- ▪ *Timing of interventions*: Too early and the issue can fail to be understood, too late and the opportunity for learning may be lost. In making an intervention, the facilitator asks of themselves *"Should I?"*, *"Could I?"* and *"Would I?"*.
- ▪ *Being truthfully helpful*: Structuring statements to be of maximum benefit to individuals and to the set as a whole.
- ▪ *Saying nothing and being invisible*: Sometimes to intervene at critical points may short-circuit the learning process of a set member or the entire set.
- ▪ *Calibrating action and learning*: When set members dwell on what they have learned, the facilitator may need to ask *"So, what are you going to do?"*. When the bulk of the talk is about action, the facilitator may need to enquire *"So what is this saying to you?"*

What is not needed are expert *"trainer"* skills, where the content of set meetings is predefined and time is rigidly structured into watertight sessions; where presentation skills which place set members into a passive role are welcomed and where oratorical fluency, which can suggest inauthenticity is valued.

Desirable Facilitator Experience

- ▪ *Having been an action learning set member*: This would be a sine qua non so that the facilitator had *"been there, done that, got the T-shirt"*.
- ▪ *Having facilitated a variety of sets*: The wider the variety, the greater the exposure, and so more comprehensive the experience.
- ▪ *A portfolio of formal and informal evidence*: Evidence of evaluation reports, journal articles and testimonials.
- ▪ *Having a supervisory relationship*: This could be on a one-to-one basis or a group basis, such as membership of a facilitated set of action learning facilitators.
- ▪ *Useful models*: Drawing, where appropriate, on those models and frameworks that can illustrate what is happening in a set and/or in the workplace. Material from literature and poetry can be useful here too.
- ▪ *A range of tools*: For use in set meetings and for set members in work settings, to help individuals and the set when they appear to be *"stuck"*.

A Facilitator's Checklist

These are among the things that a facilitator would need to consider when asked to facilitate a set.

- *Who is the client*: Who are the major stakeholders and what exactly are their expectations?
- *What variant of action learning is being called for*: This may involve discussing the different alternatives with the client.
- *What are the intended outcomes*: How clear is it what action learning is expected to achieve? How realistic is this expectation?
- *The match between the organisational culture and the underlying assumptions of action learning*: If there is a mismatch, should action learning even be considered at all?
- *A strategic or operational intervention*: Is the focus to be on small-scale operational concerns or bigger, longer-term strategic imperatives? Or both?
- *Tame or wicked issues*: What is the likely balance between these?
- *Who are the champions*: Do they exist? If not, can such an individual or a group be identified, briefed and mobilised?
- *The entry process*: To what extent are set members and their sponsors realistically prepared for what is to come by their involvement in action learning?
- *The re-entry process*: When the set ends are there arrangements in place for capitalising on the learning achieved? Is there a pre-prepared strategy for this or is help needed in developing one?
- *Voluntary and diverse set membership*: Criteria for set membership may need to be discussed with the client.
- *Venue(s)*: For face-to-face set meetings a quiet place or places with no interruptions, comfortable chairs, flipcharts, pads, pens, tea and coffee all arranged. For virtual set meetings the requirements highlighted in Chapter 5 are needed.
- *Frequency and duration of set meetings*: This needs to be clarified at the outset.
- *Evaluation*: Rather than retrospectively, this needs to be considered at the beginning.

Facilitator Development

There are three major routes for the development of facilitators.

- *Self-development*: This involves development by way of personal experience, observation, co-facilitation, coaching, mentoring by an experienced facilitator, reflective practice, reading and writing, rather than by a formal programme. There is no validation by an external body.

This is a route by which many facilitators start, and it can be successful, especially where the person concerned has access to the relevant support.

■ ***Proprietary or private training***: Delivered through a taught programme based on an in-house model or approach. These are usually focused on the more practical aspects of action learning and the practice methods approved by the delivering organisation. These may lead to an in-house award, recognised by an awarding organisation such as the UK's Institute of Leadership and Management (ILM) or the US-initiated World Institute of Action Learning (WIAL). This route is problematic in terms of quality control as, given the range of different preferences for models and approaches, it can be difficult to identify which approach to action learning is being offered.

■ ***Qualifications recognised by a statutory body***: This usually comprises a taught programme based on a recognised framework or standards and the route takes a broader approach in understanding the different perspectives and variants, coupled with critical reflection on personal practice, together with guided study on underpinning concepts and theory. This approach leads to formally assessed and accredited qualifications, such as the standards for action learning facilitators regulated by the UK's Office of Qualifications and Examinations Regulation (OFQUAL) and as offered by the ILM. Also falling within this route are university-accredited programmes that map to the standards set by the UK's Advance HE.

However, it is possible that many *"certified"* action learning facilitators may be lacking in competence to facilitate sets effectively and that many effectual facilitators are *"naturals"* who bring to the role a mixture of intuitiveness and reflection on their experience (4). Certification and accreditation do not, in practice, necessarily guarantee competence.

Even if the latter two routes are followed, continuing self-development by a facilitator remains a constant important factor. This can be done by a variety of means, including:

■ Assessing personal strengths and areas for potential improvement by seeking feedback from set members, colleagues and mentors and by reflecting on experiences, challenges and successes.

■ Attending conferences, courses, workshops, webinars and other events that offer fresh insights, skills and approaches.

■ Participating in networks and communities of practice that offer peer support.

■ Reading books, journal articles, accounts of practice, blogs and accessing podcasts.

- Writing a personal journal or learning diary for self-reflection as a basis for eventual publication.
- Maintaining well-being and balance by taking care of physical, mental, emotional and spiritual health and by managing levels of stress, fatigue and burn-out. This involves setting healthy boundaries and limits, identifying expectations for self and others and finding means of relaxing, recharging and enjoying life outside of work situations (5).
- Seeking supervision from other experienced facilitators who can offer feedback, support and, where necessary, guidance. This may involve engaging in regular supervision sessions, either individually or in a group, where challenges, dilemmas and questions can be addressed with a supervisor or peers.

Some of these possibilities are considered further in Chapter 15. There is also the means of a *"meta-set"*, comprising existing facilitators alone, whose challenges relate to the work of facilitating other sets. This can be a powerful way of pursuing self-development as well as providing a form of supervision (6).

The whole question of the professionalisation of action learning facilitators is a problematic one. The related field of coaching offers an interesting comparison because it has become increasingly professionalised and codified, with the creation of several competing professional bodies, the establishment of credentials, competency grids and supervisory regimes (7). Action learning is instead probably best regarded as an open field of practice (8) – a source of expressive and creative action, rather than as a functional discipline or profession, not least because it draws upon and borrows from many other fields which give it added depth and complexity. As such an open field with *"fuzzy"* boundaries it is probably incapable of being put into any kind of single fixed competency framework because it values both intuition and reflexivity; spawns a range of different varieties and is constantly evolving. This openness originates with Revans who asserted that the day he had to define action learning in words would be the day that he would have nothing more to do with it and, while citing many action learning principles, he preferred to focus on *"what action learning is not"* (9) and this has been successively amplified (10). This lack of definition allows action learning to *"mean different things to different people"* (11) and so its meaning can therefore usefully emerge and re-emerge from the intersection of practice and theory (12). Nevertheless, there have been some calls for greater definition and an ethical framework for action learning practice (13) as a means of self-regulation, involving such factors as confidentiality, avoidance of conflicts of interest, recognition and continual enhancement of competence.

References

1. Duch, B., Groh, S. and Allen, D. (2001) *The Power of Problem-Based Learning*, Sterling, VA: Stylus
2. Rigg, C. (2006) Action Learning in the Public Service System: Issues, Tensions and a Future Agenda, in Rigg, C. and Richards, S. (Eds.) *Organisational Development in Public Services*, Abingdon: Routledge, 195–206
3. Hauser, B., Rigg, C., Trehan, K. and Vince, R. (2023) How to Facilitate Critical Action Learning, *Action Learning: Research and Practice*, 20 (2): 116–131
4. Claxton, G. (2000) The Anatomy of Intuition, in Atkinson, T. and Claxton, G. (Eds.) *The Intuitive Practitioner: Or the Value of Not Always Knowing What One Is Doing*, Buckingham: Open University Press
5. Csikszentmihaly, M. (1990) *Flow: The Psychology of Happiness*, London: Rider
6. Mead, G. (2006) Developing Ourselves as Police Leaders: How Can We Enquire Collaboratively in Hierarchical Organisations? in Rigg, C. and Richards, S. (Eds.) *Organisational Development in Public Services*, Abingdon: Routledge, 117–213
7. Doherty, D. (2016) The Evolution of One Practitioner's Coach Approach: Taking the Coaching Turn, *Philosophy of Coaching: An International Journal*, 1 (1): 21–35
8. Cooper, R. (1976) The Open Field, *Human Relations*, 29 (11): 999–1017
9. Revans, R. (2011) *The ABC of Action Learning*, Farnham: Gower Publishing
10. Simpson, P. and Bourner, T. (2007) What Action Learning Is Not in the Twenty-First Century, *Action Learning: Research & Practice*, 4 (2): 173–187
11. Weinstein, K. (1995) *Action Learning: A Journey in Discovery and Development*, London: Harper Collins
12. Clark, E. (2009) *Action Learning Within a British Business School: Meeting the Challenge and Grasping the Opportunity*, Paper Presented at Organisational Learning, Knowledge and Capabilities (OLKC) conference, April 26–28, University of Warwick
13. Johnson, C. (2010) A Framework for the Ethical Practice of Action Learning, *Action Learning: Research and Practice*, 7 (3): 267–283

Chapter 12

Action Learning Organisation-Wide

Action learning can, at first sight, appear to be largely an individual-focused activity. Yet it has been suggested (1) that every individual has within their gift, through their reflexive awareness and ability to act differently, both individually and collectively, the capacity to shape and reshape the organisational and social setting in which they find themselves. Similarly, it has been proposed that *"it is through the questioning and awareness-raising processes that can produce changes of heart and mind where the near-invisible processes of change can begin"* (2). This can be seen in contrast to predominant top-down and cascaded *"grand narrative"* Organisation Development (OD) programmes where, at best, learning and change are, in practice, limited to isolated pockets or cultural islands and are often blocked by numerous barriers and boundaries to transmission and exchange (3). What is needed are means of avoiding ad hoc and short-term initiatives with limited reach and scope and a widening of the circles of inclusivity (4,5). This approach has been described (6) as being *"rhizomatic"* – involving a variety of relationships and associations that extend in both space and time to form a gigantic, intricate and evolving texture of dependencies and references.

The organisation-wide ambit of action learning, in turn, relates to:

- The willingness of the senior people in an organisation to promote individual and organisational learning and to make the necessary resources available to achieve this.

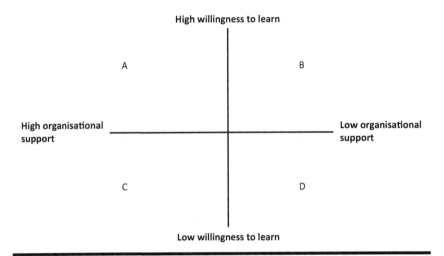

Figure 12.1   Learning and organisational support.

- The willingness of individuals to approach new learning in a positive and welcoming spirit.

Figure 12.1 illustrates how these two dimensions open up a number of possibilities:

In Quadrant A there would be a high commitment among staff to new learning opportunities, with a willingness to take risks and to be challenged – clearly a fruitful context for action learning. Quadrant B defines those situations where staff would be prone to develop a cynical attitude to the few development activities that might be on offer, or alternatively, a sense of frustration and anger when denied any development opportunities. Quadrant C is where senior organisational leadership is committed to learning and change but staff appear not to be so, and simply rely on their existing skills and knowledge, demonstrating anxiety about the prospect of change. Quadrant D is an organisational culture of *"non-learning"* (7) and *"trained incapacity"* (8) where there is no reflection on experience and no effort to examine current practices.

There are major barriers or defences that serve to prevent individual and organisational learning, most of which are grounded in an overriding bias for action, with more value being associated with action and results than with reflection and inquiry. The ability to always promote decisive and directive action in the face of uncertainty is highly valued. Where the dominant goal is to always reach out quickly for decisions and make something happen this produces a form of *"hurry sickness"* (9) where people feel chronically short of time, tend to try to perform every task faster and get anxious and flustered when encountering any delay.

Revans advanced the principle of insufficient mandate, where *"Those unable to change themselves cannot change what goes on around them"* (10), so action was seen as being the servant of learning and so serves as a motivator for it. Action is regarded as both an input to learning and an output from it, so a major challenge is to achieve an appropriate balance between an organisational (action) focus and an individual (learning) focus.

Preparation and Design

Before action learning is adopted in an organisation the culture and climate of the organisation needs to be assessed, as suggested by Figure 12.1. Chapter 4 addresses this requirement. The key questions are:

- Does the organisation really want to do it?
- Does it face a compelling strategic challenge that has been well-articulated?
- Is the organisation really in a place where it is ready to do it?
- Are there compelling reasons for people to change how they relate to one another and develop new networks of relationships?
- Is there a desire within the organisation to increase its learning capacity?
- Are senior leaders and managers in the organisation willing to change their own behaviour?
- Are those people willing to support the development of people through providing feedback and engaging in dialogue? (11)

The focus would then be on the initiation and formation processes before sets begin to be formed and then meet. This is patient and time-consuming work to develop a *"structure of welcome"* (12). This may be undertaken by the facilitator or by a senior organisational leader taking on the role of *"accoucheur"* or midwife to help action learning to emerge. It is like the role of *"tolkatch"* – a networker, middleman, broker, fixer and dealmaker (13). This is also much like the UK Design Council's characteristics of *"changemakers"* – systems thinkers, designers, storytellers, connectors and convenors (14).

Learning Architecture

A learning architecture is the way that an organisation promotes and structures individual and organisational learning (15). It involves tying together and aligning those learning initiatives previously being considered as being solely tactical in nature and/or confined to specific staff groups. It involves the mechanisms for sharing the learning which emerges across an organisation or organisations in a systematic, system-wide and coordinated way. The creation or development of a learning architecture is important because the promotion and facilitation of personal and organisational learning requires its own strategy and structure and without such an approach learning will be confined only to isolated pockets of activity.

Three examples of learning architecture development are:

- A review of working with action learning in healthcare (16) identified the factors that needed to be in place for the impact of action learning to extend beyond the set. The organisation needed to take a strategic approach to the setting up of sets and to link them to other relevant activities and networks. Sets needed to be aware of the wider context within which they were working, including who and what they needed to influence and how best to do this. An influential person in the wider system had to take a close and supportive interest in what sets were doing and help them, where appropriate, to grapple with issues.

- In a study of action learning for organisation development in South Korean companies (17), the key factors identified included top management support, a clear understanding of local culture, the macro-management of a series of action learning sets and the effective use of facilitators.

- Action learning was linked to large whole system change conferences (18). Dialogue and collective engagement were mobilised between several sets *("a structure that reflects")* and large change conferences *("a structure that connects")*, the latter being a space where reflection was linked to power. The process required the active engagement of key decision-makers to move beyond mere leadership rhetoric.

The aim of a learning architecture is to permanently embed the action learning process within continuing cycles of organisational review, planning and learning – to hard-wire learning into organisational systems, policies and procedures. There can be no standard blueprint for the design of a learning architecture because it will need to reflect the circumstances and nature of the organisation concerned, the context within which it operates and the key stakeholders and partners. While taking the context into account, it must remain adaptable to external changes as well as those arising from the action learning process (4,19). What is clear is that it implies major change to pre-existing education and training and performance management systems (15), as well as the decision-making processes used, the permeability of boundaries with other organisations and responsiveness to customers/clients (16). As the nature of a learning architecture will be both collaborative and collective, the process by which it is designed should also be collaborative and should involve all the significant stakeholders. Unless there is such a collaborative effort it is unlikely that the learning architecture designed will have the ownership which would be essential for success.

The underlying values for a learning architecture are (20):

- ■ *Openness*: The sharing of learning emphasises informal channels and personal contacts over any written reporting procedures, so cross-discipline groupings and the planned rotation of staff are ingredients.
- ■ *Trust*: For people to give of their best, take appropriate risks and develop their capacity, they must trust that such activities will be appreciated and valued. Specifically, they must be confident that should they err, they will be supported, rather than castigated.
- ■ *Belief in human potential*: People are valued for their creativity, energy and innovation, so their personal and organisational development are cherished and fostered.
- ■ *Tolerance of mistakes*: Learning from failure as well as success is a prerequisite for development and this implies accepting the positive spin-offs from errors, rather than blaming or scapegoating.
- ■ **Absence of complacency**: Innovation and change are valued across the organisation and involves identifying current good practice and encouraging its amplification.
- ■ *Recognition of tacit knowledge*: People who are closest to the action have the best understanding concerning potential and flaws. Such tacit knowledge is valued and there is an enlargement of their discretion, responsibility and capability.
- ■ *Celebration of success*: If excellence is to be pursued with commitment, then its attainment must be valued across the organisational culture.

In one sense this is not new. Revans was always clear that action learning was just as much about learning and development organisation-wide as it was for individuals (21).

References

1. Cole, M. (2020) *Radical Organisation Development*, Abingdon: Routledge
2. Pedler, M. (2020) On Social Action, *Action Learning: Research & Practice*, 17 (1): 1–9
3. Bussu, S. and Marshall, M. (2020) Organisational Development to Support Integrated Care in East London: The Perspectives of Clinicians and Social Workers on the Ground, *Journal of Health Organisation and Management*, 34 (5): 603–619

4. Attwood, M., Pedler, M., Pritchard, S. and Wilkinson, D. (2003) *Leading Change: A Guide to Whole Systems Working*, Bristol, MA: Polity Press
5. Freedman, A. (2011) Using Action Learning for Organisation Development and Change, *OD Practitioner*, 43 (2): 7–13
6. Nicolini, D. (2013) *Practice Theory, Work and Organisation*, Oxford: Oxford University Press
7. Marsick, V. and Watkins, K. (1990) *Informal and Incidental Learning in the Workplace*, London: Routledge
8. Merton, R. (1958) *Bureaucratic Structure and Personality in Social Theory and Social Structure*, Glencoe, IL: The Free Press
9. Friedman, H. and Booth-Kewley, S. (1987) Personality, Type A Behaviour and Coronary Heart Disease: The Role of Emotional Expression, *Journal of Personality and Social Psychology*, 53 (4): 783–792
10. Revans, R. (2011) *The ABC of Action Learning*, Farnham: Gower Publishing
11. Yorks, L., Lamm, S. and O'Neil, J. (1999) Transfer of Learning from Action Learning Programs to the Organisational Setting, in Yorks, L., O'Neil, J. and Marsick, V. (Eds.) *Action Learning: Successful Strategies for Individual, Team and Organisational Development, Advances in Developing Human Resources, 2*, San Francisco, CA: Berrett-Koehler, 56–74
12. Revans, R. (1982) *The Origins and Growth of Action Learning*, Bromley: Chartwell-Bratt
13. Schon, D. (1973) *Beyond the Stable State: Public and Private Learning in a Changing Society*, Harmondsworth: Penguin
14. www.designcouncil.org.uk/our-resources/systemic-design-framework/
15. Pedler, M., Warburton, D. and Wilkinson, D. (2007) *Improving Poor Environments: The Role of Learning Architectures in Developing and Spreading Good Practice*, Bristol: Environment Agency
16. Edmonstone, J. (2011) Action Learning and Organisation Development, in Pedler, M. (Ed.) *Action Learning in Practice*, 4th edition, Farnham: Gower, 285–295
17. Cho, Y. and Bong, H-C. (2011) Action Learning for Organisation Development in South Korea, in Pedler, M. (Ed.) *Action Learning in Practice*, 4th edition Farnham: Gower, 249–260
19. Pedler, M. and Attwood, M. (2011) How Can Action Learning Contribute to Social Capital? *Action Learning: Research & Practice*, 8 (1): 27–39
18. Nicolini, D., Sher, M., Childerstone, S. and Gorli, M. (2004) In Search of the "Structure that Reflects": Promoting Organisational Reflection Practices in a UK Health Authority, in Reynolds, M. & Vince, R. (Eds.) *Organising Reflection*, Aldershot: Ashgate Publishing, 43–55
20. Davies, H. and Nutley, S. (2004) Organisations as Learning Systems, in Kernick, D. (Ed.) *Complexity and Healthcare Organisations: A View from the Street*, Abingdon: Radcliffe Medical Press, 59–68
21. Revans, R. (1982) *The Enterprise as a Learning System, in the Origins and Growth of Action Learning*, Bromley: Chartwell-Bratt, 280–286

Chapter 13

Action Learning and Culture

Culture is *"the set of customs, traditions and values of a society or community such as a nation or ethnic group, which bind people together, acquired over time and transmitted through processes of social learning, from one generation to the next"* (1). Action learning has been described as both a pragmatic methodology for dealing with difficult challenges, but also a moral philosophy based on an optimistic view of human potential (2). In the case of the latter, it has drawn strongly upon Christian, Quaker and Buddhist ideals and values (3,4). As action learning has spread globally and is used in at least seventy member states of the United Nations in Europe, Asia, the Middle East, North, Central and South America, Africa and the Pacific in both private and public sector organisations (5) the question of how it relates to people and organisations who do not necessarily share the same value set has become ever more important.

Everyone is embedded in their local culture and that culture is embedded in everyone (6) in a kind of collective programming of the mind. Attempts have been made to map different national cultures (7,8), but the dangers of doing so have become clear. For example:

- Individuals have multiple cultural identities, so the importance of one identity need not obliterate the importance of the others (9).
- National cultures are never uniform but are necessarily pluralistic in nature, involving shifting sub-cultures.
- Cultures do not remain static but change through time.

DOI: 10.4324/9781003464440-13

■ They are not bounded by national borders and borders themselves change through time.
■ Gender differences are typically not taken into consideration.

Much of the commentary on action learning has been (and continues to be) delivered through a prism of Western values which assume a set of human universals – distinctive beliefs about human nature that form the bedrock of Western thought and are silently assumed to be those that drive people all over the world and throughout all of history (10). Yet the notion of a universal value set and associated norms of behaviour have increasingly been challenged (11,12), especially by China which refers to it caustically as *"Western universalism"*. Evidence from action learning practice from around the world provides examples of it being used in ways that do not necessarily reflect such Western values. For example, it has been adopted as a method or technique without any attention to the underlying ethos (13). There are cases of deep-rooted and institutionalised preferences for teacher-centred learning approaches (14) and of the influence of religious and gender-based cultural norms (15). In other cultures, there is a strong deference to age and authority and there are different perceptions of time and commitment (16).

Rather than any comparative *"mapping"* approaches to culture it is likely that cultural anthropology and ethnography offer more nuanced approaches to understanding cultural differences because they consider culture to be more expansive and inclusive and are power-sensitive, focusing on the continuing impact of historical circumstances such as gender, slavery and colonialism. From this perspective, cultural relationships are viewed as being underpinned by power dynamics, where all the parties to interactions do not experience the relationship as being an equal one. This is particularly important in relation to those countries such as Portugal, Spain, Italy, Belgium, France and Germany and the nations which succeeded colonial rule – but especially in relation to the UK – as *"In no other contemporary nation-state does imperial nationalism endure with such explicit social, political and economic consequences"* (17).

There are two important areas where the fostering of a cultural sensitivity is important – that of international students studying in Western higher education institutions where action learning forms part of a blended programme, and the adoption of action learning in non-Western countries.

International Students

For international students studying in Master's programmes in Western countries, the higher education institutions concerned need to accept that such students will find assimilating into both a different national culture and an unfamiliar learning culture to be extremely challenging. In particular, the potential discomfort experienced by entering a learner-centred, rather than a teacher-centred, environment and the challenging possibilities of personal disclosure and of unlearning are all major factors. Moreover, the students and their parents will have funded participation in a programme and are therefore more likely to have a strong transactional attitude to delivery. Such cultural differences therefore need to be recognised early and addressed in action learning sets both at the outset of a programme of study and then continually throughout, both on a face-to-face and virtual basis. The importance of co-creation, for example of set ground rules, can embody such cultural sensitivities. An active but sensitive facilitator role in helping students address such matters as reticence and loss of face is also important (18).

Action Learning in Non-Western Contexts

In working with action learning in different cultural contexts, some rules of thumb can be identified from the evolving literature on this issue (18–20):

■ There is a need to acknowledge the existence of cultural differences and to recognise that attention to local culture is a significant and growing issue.

■ Those working with action learning need to understand their own culture by reflecting on its predominant values and beliefs before trying to understand other cultures.

■ Similarly, there is a need to recognise the tendency to default to one's own culture.

■ In some cultures, action learning may appear counter-cultural, so not necessarily attractive for everyone. Being over-evangelical about it may be self-defeating.

■ National political agendas may, in certain contexts, influence levels of receptiveness to action learning. In some settings the flexibility that set members have to act may be constrained, while in others there may be circumstances where action learning aligns well with local political interests and reform needs.

■ It is important to undertake preparation and research to try to understand, as far as possible, another culture. This might include attention to national history and any previous history of the use of action learning – of what variety? With what outcomes?

- It can be helpful to identify someone within a different culture's institutions with whom those working with action learning can collaborate to translate cultural nuances.
- It is important to invest early in relationship- and trust-building, so that action learning participants get to know and understand each other.
- Recognising differences in cultural norms is important.
  - While in Western cultures an egalitarian emphasis in a set is the norm, inviting the posing of challenges as well as offering support, in other cultures perceived authority and social status based on age, gender, class and religious affiliations and the related power differences, as well as any formal organisational hierarchy, are all potentially important.
  - In some settings asking a direct question of an authority figure could be seen as disrespectful and the Western direct, short and sharp approach to asking questions experienced as being uncomfortable.
  - In some cultures, objectivity and rationality may appear to have higher value than emotion, subjectivity or intuition and, as a result, set members may become preoccupied with problem analysis and identifying solutions, rather than enabling a set member to consider a situation freighted with uncertainty and ambiguity.
  - In some cases, people tend to agree with whatever is suggested by an authority figure and many people may feel uncomfortable citing examples of what they may have done well.
  - In some cultures, disclosing a problem or difficulty might feel shameful or risky and, as a result, other set members might feel anxious for the person concerned and want to protect them.
  - In some settings set members may seem reluctant to disclose personal challenges, rather than situational ones and regard it as unprofessional and even inappropriate to do so. Distinguishing between the personal (relating to a set member's qualities, characteristics and abilities) and the private (inappropriate to disclose) can help to define what is shareable and what is not (21).
- It is always important to demonstrate politeness and respect.
- Language should be kept as simple as possible and technical terms, jargon, colloquialisms, acronyms, abbreviations, slang and the use of metaphors that have different meanings or connotations in different cultures should be avoided.
- It is advisable to be careful with the use of humour, which does not necessarily translate well across cultures.
- It is valuable to seek feedback, both formally and informally, and adjust accordingly.

▪ The development of action learning facilitators needs to include attention to cultural and political awareness.

In practice, there needs to be a form of mutual adjustment between the Western-originated values of action learning and those of a local culture. So, action learning itself needs to be responsive to change and be open to influence. The elastic nature of action learning is already evident in the multiple variants described in Chapter 3 and the ability to easily and frequently change has led to action learning being described as a *"protean practice"* (22). A description of action learning in an international development and relief organisation concluded that allowing a variety of action learning models to emerge and develop enabled achievement of a broad range of benefits (23) while others concluded that action learning was a process that could be *"tweaked, expanded and used in different settings in different ways"* (24). Revans himself recognised the importance of cultural differences and the need for sensitivity in the way that they are addressed. He believed that flexibility was necessary in shaping action learning to both the context and the learners (25).

What seems necessary is the cultivation of a *"meta-cultural sensitivity"* (26); consider *"what are the culture aspects in that specific context with the people you have to work with?"* (27). This has also been described as Cultural Intelligence or CQ (28). Lee (29) identified action learning as an essential tool in such cross-cultural provision and saw it as an approach which *"Specifically allows/requires an explicit investigation of conflicting micro- and macro-cultural norms, both as they are perceived to exist, and as they are dynamically co-regulated"*.

References

1. Edmonstone, J. (2022) *Organisation Development in Healthcare: A Critical Appraisal for Practitioners*, Abingdon: Routledge
2. Pedler, M. and Abbott, C. (2013) *Facilitating Action Learning: A Practitioner's Guide*, Maidenhead: McGraw-Hill/Open University Press
3. Boshyk, Y. (2011) Ad Fontes: Reg Revans: Some Early Sources of His Personal Growth and Values, in Pedler, M. (Ed.) *Action Learning in Practice*, 4th edition, Farnham: Gower Publishing, 81–91
4. Revans, R. (1982) The Immemorial Precursor: Action Learning Past and Present, in Revans, R. (Ed.) *The Origins and Growth of Action Learning*, Bromley: Chartwell-Bratt, 529–545
5. Boshyk, Y. (Ed.) (2002) *Action Learning Worldwide: Experiences of Leadership and Organisational Development*, Farnham: Gower Publishing
6. Ryde, J. (2019) *White Privilege Unmasked: How to be Part of the Solution*, London: Jessica Kingsley

7. Joy, S. and Kolb, D. (2009) Are There Cultural Differences in Learning Style? *International Journal of Cultural Relations*, 33 (1): 69–85

8. Hofstede, G. (2001) *Culture's Consequences: Comparing Values, Behaviours, Institutions and Organisations Across Nations*, Thousand Oaks, CA: Sage Publications

9. Sen, A. (2006) *Identity and Violence: The Illusion of Destiny*, London: Penguin

10. Lent, J. (2017) *The Patterning Instinct: A Cultural History of Humanity's Search for Meaning*, Amherst, NY: Prometheus Books

11. Ricketts, P. (2022) *Hard Choices: The Making and Understanding of Global Britain*, London: Atlantic Books

12. Mason, P. (2021) *How to Stop Fascism: History: Ideology: Resistance*, London: Penguin Books

13. Burger, U. and Trehan, K. (2018) Action Learning in East Africa: New Encounters or Impossible Challenges? *Action Learning: Research & Practice*, 15 (2): 126–138

14. Edmonstone, J. and Robson, J. (2013) Blending-In: The Contribution of Action Learning to a Master's Programme in Human Resources in Health, *International Journal of Human Resource Development and Management*, 13 (1): 61–75

15. Mughal, F., Gatrell, C. and Stead, V. (2018) Cultural Politics and the Role of the Action Learning Facilitator: Analysing the Negotiation of Critical Action Learning in the Pakistani MBA Through a Bourdieusian Lens, *Management Learning*, 49 (1): 69–85

16. Stevens, G. and de Vera, M. (2015) Action Learning: Cultural Differences, *Action Learning: Research & Practice*, 12 (2): 215–223

17. Elkins, C. (2023) *Legacy of Violence: A History of the British Empire*, London: Vintage

18. Edmonstone, J. (2019) Is Action Learning Culture-Bound? An Exploration, *Action Learning: Research & Practice*, 16 (3): 223–237

19. Dilworth, R. and Boshyk, Y. (2010) Action Learning in Different National and Organisational Contexts and Cultures, in Boshyk, Y. and Dilworth, R. (Eds.) *Action Learning: History and Evolution*, Basingstoke: Palgrave Macmillan, 205–233

20. Wright, N. (2021) Cross-Cultural Action Learning, www.actionlearning associates.co.uk/cross-cultural-action-learning/

21. Fook, J. and Askeland, A. (2007) Challenges of Critical Reflection: "Nothing Ventured, Nothing Gained", *Social Work Education*, 28 (5): 520–533

22. Brook, C., Pedler, M. and Burgoyne, J. (2012) A Protean Practice: Perspectives on the Practice of Action Learning, *European Journal of Training and Development*, 37 (8): 728–743

23. Wright, N. (2004) Using Action Learning to Support Individual and Organisational Reflection in an International Development and Relief Agency, *Action Learning: Research & Practice*, 1 (1): 81–89

24. Lustig, P. and Rai, D. (2009) Action Learning in ActionAid Nepal: A Case Study, *Action Learning: Research & Practice*, 6 (2): 165–169

25. Revans, R. (1982) *The Nile Project, in Revans, R. The Origins and Growth of Action Learning*, Bromley: Chartwell-Bratt, 372–425

26. Louie, K. (2005) Gathering Cultural Knowledge: Useful or Handle with Care? in Carroll, J. and Ryan, J. (Eds.) *Teaching International Students: Improved Learning for All*, London: Routledge, 92–103

27. Loeve, M. (2007) Mind-set Change in a Cross-Cultural Context, *Action Learning: Research and Practice*, 4 (2): 211–218

28. Livermore, D., Van Dyne, L. and Ang, S. (2022) Organisational CQ: Cultural Intelligence for 21st Century Organisations, *Business Horizons*, 65 (5): 671–680

29. Lee, M. (1996) Action Learning as a Cross-Cultural Tool, in Stewart, J. and McGoldrick, J. (Eds.) *Human Resource Development: Perspectives, Strategies and Practice*, London: Pitman , 64–72

Chapter 14

Evaluating Action Learning

Action learning has benefits at individual, organisational and social levels, but it is important, although challenging, to identify these and to learn what works well and what does not.

- ### *What is evaluation for?*
  Evaluation is about learning and the consequential taking of appropriate action. It has been noted (1) that *"We cannot regard truth as a goal of inquiry. The purpose of inquiry is to achieve agreement among human beings about what to do, to bring consensus on the end to be achieved and the means to be used to achieve those ends. Inquiry that does not achieve coordination of behaviour is not inquiry but simply wordplay"*. Likewise, a survey identifying learning from evaluation studies (2) concluded that *"Evaluation can only ever provide good quality information to inform decision-making. It is unlikely to supply ready-made answers because the results will need to be interpreted as part of a process of discussion and judgement, with the views of different stakeholders and the intended outcomes of the activity taken into account"*. It is concerned with how we generalise from the past into the future (3). Evaluation increasingly takes place in an organisational and social setting where *"nothing is clear, and everything keeps changing"* (4) because there will be large parts of the system being evaluated that are not known or understood, at least at the outset. So, the notion of *"rational"* or straightforward application of evidence in making choices is necessarily either flawed or naïve. A whole

 DOI: 10.4324/9781003464440-14

range of factors impact on human behaviour, so trying to narrow it down in this way is an enormous over-simplification. Evaluation involves trade-offs, often between competing values and judgement calls. These are normative debates, where facts and values interact. So, evaluation is about creating opportunities for stepping back, reflecting, learning and sense-making, and through this achievement of greater awareness, understanding and action. Accordingly, evaluation activity is an intervention itself.

▪ *Problems with evaluation*

There is almost universal agreement on the importance and value of evaluation, but it is important to identify at the outset a distinction between two major types:

• *Summative* (or judgemental) evaluation is concerned with justifying the investment in (mostly) financial terms and with assessing the overall outcomes – the measurable impact or contribution, and so is more likely to be valued by funders and budget-holders, to rely on *"hard"* data and to require quick answers. The major concern will be to review costs and benefits and so ensure value for the investment made.

• *Formative* (or developmental) evaluation is concerned with improvement and steering and so serves to reinforce learning. It is focused on process, rather than outcomes, so is more likely to be favoured by those concerned with individual and organisational development, who value the rich information accrued, including the impact of context or setting on learning.

The distinction between the two types is shown in Table 14.1.

The quantitative approach exemplified by summative evaluation may not just be undesirable for certain human activities, but perhaps even impossible (5).

Table 14.1 Summative and Formative Evaluation

	Summative	*Formative evaluation*
Goal	Truth and scientific acceptance	Understanding and perspective
Measurement	Quantitative data	Qualitative data
Evaluator approach	Objectivity	Subjectivity
Relationships	Distance and detachment	Closeness and involvement
Inquiry mode	Deduction	Induction
Outcomes	Generalisations	Context-bound conclusion

To measure anything an objective yardstick is needed such as centimetres for length or kilometres for distance. Human activity at work involves a range of complex tasks that are highly context-dependent, so it may well be a fallacy to believe that such activity can be measured objectively using a yardstick and so result in hard figures. Measurement of this kind tends to use Likert scales, which involve respondents rating statements by selecting from a range of possible responses (such as poor, adequate, good and very good) or figures (often as –2, –1, 0, +1 and +2). These are intuitive approximations based on subjective criteria and so any translation of results into figures serves to create a false impression of objective quantifiability.

There are two major summative evaluation approaches – the **Kirkpatrick Four Levels** model (6) and the **Return on Investment** (ROI) methodology (7).

With the ladder-like or *"chain reaction"* Kirkpatrick model evaluation is considered at four levels:

- **Reaction**: This asks to what degree participants reacted favourably to the learning event in terms of their thoughts and feelings. It is the level of the *"happy sheet"* administered to a captive audience at the end of an event and is the most common form of assessment used. It gives a brief glimpse of how learners intend to apply their learning, but the findings at this level are rarely followed up.

  It is then slightly more difficult, but not impossible to collect data.

- **Learning**: This asks to what degree participants acquired the intended knowledge, skills and attitudes, based on their participation in the learning event.

  It is then even more problematic to collect data on resulting changes in behaviour.

- **Behaviour**: This asks to what degree participants apply what they have learned from the learning event when back in the work setting.

  It is then very difficult indeed to collect data.

- **Outcomes or results**: This asks to what degree desired outcomes occur because of the learning event – the effect of changed behaviour on performance.

The movement from reactions to outcomes introduces a significant number of intervening variables (or other things happening to the individuals and/or the organisations concerned) which make it difficult to ascribe a simple cause-and-effect relationship. It is thus very difficult to measure learning transfer – what learners attempt to apply when they return to their normal work environment (8). Moreover, the correlation between the levels is weak – a positive result at one level does not necessarily lead to a positive result at the next. By concentrating on the relatively easy-to-assess participant reactions, the tendency is to sideline the contextual factors that might affect an event and its impact.

In the ROI approach, the key feature is the calculation of the monetary value of investing in an activity. The outcomes of an activity are converted into a financial value, enabling a cost-benefit analysis to take place. Those results which cannot be monetised are called *"intangibles"*. Only financial quantitative data really matters and intangibles, as evidenced by qualitative data, are relegated to a secondary role. As a result, ROI risks either minimising such results or forcing an essentially hypothetical and subjective financial value on them. Yet such intangibles can clearly lead to significant benefits over time (9). While calculating the costs of a programme are relatively easy, if somewhat time-consuming and disputable, a real challenge lies in defining the gains made (10).

Both approaches are based on a supposedly scientific approach – set objectives, apply intervention, isolate effects of intervention and measure results. Yet how appropriate is this where there are multiple variables and where human agency plays a major role in determining outcomes?

There are other problems associated with evaluation (11), including:

- **Time**: How to evaluate initiatives over the short term that are intended to have much longer-term impacts?
- **Context**: What works in one setting may not necessarily work in another. Factors such as culture, values, timing, priorities and attitudes all play their part.
- **Complexity**: Given the multiple intervening variables, how can the effect of one activity be disentangled from the others, especially when they may overlap?
- **Value**: What counts as *"success"*? What is valued and by whom? Who are the key stakeholders and what are they seeking to achieve?
- **Horses for courses**: The size and complexity of an evaluation exercise needs to be in proportion to the activity being evaluated and the form the evaluation takes should, in turn, reflect the values underlying the activity itself.
- **Cost**: Conducting evaluation is not cost-free. It will involve additional work, with associated costs, whether sourced internally or externally. Ideally, evaluation and the associated costs should be planned for at the outset, but in practice, this rarely happens, and evaluation is usually conducted retrospectively, often as an afterthought.
- **Politics**: Evaluation is a complex and highly political process. Policy decisions are sometimes made despite evidence of what does or does not work in practice. Evaluation can be used to gather data that supports a particular policy direction – policy-based evidence, rather than evidence-based policy. If evaluation work results in an *"unacceptable finding"* and is sensitive politically, they may never see the light of day

and may be ignored. Decisions are made on much more than evaluation evidence – values, interests, personalities, timing, circumstances and happenstance all also play their parts.

■ *Evaluating action learning*

Action learning is recognised as comprising both an ethos and a method (or series of methods) yet evaluation typically focuses only on action learning as a method. If an organisation's culture does not match or reflect the ethos, then action learning may be seen as a counter-cultural *"island"* and so easily dismissed. Ideally, therefore, there should be a degree of *"fit"* between an organisation's culture and action learning. This is addressed in Chapter 12.

Action learning is open-ended and unpredictable in nature. It is difficult, probably even impossible, to predict specific outcomes from action learning in advance and in detail. Therefore, action learning can potentially lead to the unexpected and possibly surprising. The presenting problem that set members bring may well change or evolve from interactions and dialogue with other set members. The challenges set members face will be highly individual in nature and not all the issues involved can be predicted in advance. Even where action learning is focused on a single overall theme or project, the challenges which set members encounter may be unexpected and highly individual. Inherent in action learning, therefore, is the notion of emergence – much of the learning will emerge across a set's duration. This is unlike more conventional *"training"* approaches which seek to constrain uncertainty and aim to establish order through curricula and application of techniques (12). Moreover, action learning works largely through generative causation (creating conditions where things can change and move on to destinations yet unknown) rather than successionist causation (achieving predictable and pre-known outcomes) (13).

Another difficulty in evaluating action learning lies with the multiplicity of stakeholders. Each set member may have different perceptions and intentions regarding their issues they bring and the set itself – and these may change over the set's duration. Ideally, most set members will be self-directed volunteers, but this is not always the case. Each set member will have a sponsor with expectations derived from their own experience (or lack of it) of action learning and there will also be an organisational champion or champions with their own understanding of the purpose of action learning. All will have varying levels of experience and understanding and therefore have multiple expectations of desired outcomes.

■ *A way forward*

There is no *"magic bullet"* approach to evaluating action learning activity, but it will need to include both summative and formative approaches, not least because process and outcomes are, in practice, intertwined.

Formative (or in-set evaluation) should be part of the ongoing work of each set meeting. There can also be value in such activities as reviewing ground rules, the set process and the balances between support and challenge and between action and reflection. Set members might, for example, retrospectively score themselves at the beginning and end of an action learning process to benchmark change. Emergent as well as predicted outcomes could be included. Set members might evaluate what ongoing organisational factors impinged on their actions. The focus would be on evaluating progress with learning and reviewing the helpful (and less helpful) norms of the set, with a view to making further set meetings more productive. Some structured methods of conducting formative evaluation are provided in Chapter 15 – the action learning levels exercise, the action/reflection map, the set meeting review worksheet and the support/challenge map.

Summative evaluation is more challenging, but drawing on two major studies (14,15) a pre-evaluation framework is proposed based on six key areas (16).

- *Purpose:*

  What specific variant of action learning is being used, and therefore evaluated?

  How exactly is action learning being used – as an activity interwoven with other activities, as a discreet development activity or as a link between a formal programme and the workplace?

  What exactly do we want to know about the activity?

  Who are the key stakeholders? What are their expectations? What do they believe it is seeking to do?

  Is there clarity about the intended purpose and the anticipated outcomes and benefits, both individually and organisationally? Are these short or long-term?

  Are the personal and organisational development needs the activity is intended to address articulated? Are they clear? Are they retrospective or prospective?

- *Fit*

  To what extent is there *"fit"* between the values underpinning action learning and the culture of potential set members' organisation?

  Is there clarity between the underlying assumptions of the planned action learning activity and consideration of how adults learn?

- *Preparation and support*

  Is there clarity over the roles of set members, facilitators, sponsors and champions?

Are these expectations explicit or implicit? Can they be revisited when necessary?

Is there a recognised champion or champions for the action learning activity? Who are they and what is the nature of their support in practical and symbolic terms?

Will it be sustained across and beyond the activity?

How clear are set members' sponsors about the nature of action learning and the demands it is likely to make on them, on the set member and on the organisation?

Are there in place in place appropriate *"entry strategies"* to prepare set members for their involvement in action learning and the level of challenge and support that they may expect? Are there also *"re-entry strategies"* for the transition back into the workplace after action learning, where the level of support and challenge is unlikely to resemble that encountered in the set?

- *Membership*

   Is involvement in the action learning activity voluntary or directed? If the latter, what are the selection criteria for set membership?

   To what extent will biographical and other data, such as gender, age range, occupational background, level of seniority, length of time in current post and previous experience of action learning be collected as part of an evaluation?

- *Issues*

   Are the issues which set members will address tame or wicked problems, or both?

   How much choice or prescription is there for set members' choice of issue?

   Who decides on the issues to be addressed?

- *Steering*

   Are there effective arrangements in place for steering the action learning activity and reviewing and modifying it where necessary?

   How much flexibility is there in design terms? Can real-time changes be easily made?

- *Evaluation process*

   Who is the evaluation information for?

   When will the information be needed?

   In what form will it be needed?

   How will the information be collected and analysed? By whom?

What will the product of the evaluation process be?

What are the resource implications of the evaluation in terms of finance and time?

Will the benefits of the evaluation outweigh the costs of undertaking it?

Will the evaluation contribute to an evidence-base of *"What works, in what circumstances and why?"* Will it move matters forward?

Raelin (17) has further suggested that evaluation itself should focus on:

- *Effort*

  What was the cost of the action learning activity?

  How many people participated?

  How much time did it take?

  Who sponsored the activity and what were their expectations?

- *Process*

  What need is the action learning activity responding to?

  How is the presenting problem or problems being addressed?

  What were the distinguishing features of the action learning activity?

  Which issues were chosen and how?

- *Short-term performance*

  What was addressed, changed or added?

  What were the set members reactions to their involvement?

  How did the other stakeholders react to the action learning experience?

  Did the action learning activity operate within fiancé and time budgets?

  Were there direct beneficial changes?

  Was the original need that inspired the activity met?

- *Longer-term performance*

  Have the set members changed their behaviour?

  Was there a significant change in their personal development, practices and values?

  Did involvement lead to career change or advancement for set members?

  Have there been effects from involvement in action learning in other parts of the organisation?

  Did the action learning activity in any way change the organisational culture and/or practices?

Such frameworks will involve the collection and analysis of both hard and soft data. Communicating the evaluation results is a process which is itself evaluative. For example, at the end of an action learning activity senior stakeholders (champions) may meet set members to hear about their learning and actions and, if there is a willingness, invite set members' insights into other related organisational issues. In this way evaluation becomes a more dynamic process leading to further change and influence, rather than simply resulting in a report.

References

1. Rorty, R. (1999) *Philosophy and Social Hope*, London: Penguin Books
2. Larsen, L., Cummins, J. and Brown, H. (2005) *Learning from Evaluation: Summary of Reports of Evaluations of Leadership Initiatives*, London: Office for Public Management/NHS Leadership Centre
3. Patton, M. (1997) *Utilisation-Focused Evaluation: The New Century Text*, London: Sage
4. Sharp, C. (2018) Collective Leadership: Where Nothing Is Clear and Everything Keeps Changing: Exploring New Territories for Evaluation, *Collective Leadership Scotland*, http://tinyurl.com/y6vII2hp
5. Verhaeghe, P. (2014) *What About Me? The Struggle for Identity in a Market-Based Society*, London: Scribe Publications
6. Kirkpatrick, D. and Kirkpatrick, J. (2009) *Evaluating Training Programs: The Four Levels*, 5th edition, San Francisco, CA: Berrett-Koehler
7. Phillips, J. and Phillips, P. (2008) The Basics of ROI, http://www.humanresourcesiq.com/hr-technology/column/the-basics-of-roi/
8. Huczynski, A. and Lewis, J. (1980) An Empirical Study into the Learning Transfer Process in Management Training, *Journal of Management Studies*, 17 (2): 227–240
9. Hetherton, M. (2016) *Evaluating Action Learning: Tick-Box Exercise or Powerful Change Process?* London: Action Learning Associates
10. Hardacre, J., Cragg, J., Shapiro, P., Spurgeon, P. and Flanagan, H. (2011) *What's Leadership Got to Do With It? Exploring Links Between Quality Improvement and Leadership in the NHS*, London: ORCNI for the Health Foundation
11. Edmonstone, J. (2015) The Challenge of Evaluating Action Learning, *Action Learning: Research and Practice*, 12 (2): 131–145
12. Pedler, M. and Abbott, C. (2010) *Facilitating Action Learning: A Practitioner's Guide*, Maidenhead: Open University Press/McGraw-Hill
13. Pawson, R. and Tilley, N. (1997) *Realistic Evaluation*, London: Sage
14. Hirsh, W., Tamkin, P., Garrow, V. and Burgoyne, J. (2011) *Evaluating Management and Leadership Development: New Ideas and Practical Approaches*, Brighton: Institute for Employment Studies
15. Edmonstone, J. (2013) Healthcare Leadership: Learning from Evaluation, *Leadership in Health Services*, 26 (2): 148–158
16. Edmonstone, J. (2018) *Action Learning in Health, Social and Community Care: Principles, Practices and Resources*, Boca Raton, FA: CRC Press
17. Raelin, J. (2000) *Work-Based Learning: The New Frontier of Management Development*, Upper Saddle, NJ: Prentice-Hall

Chapter 15

Action Learning Resources

Action Learning: Research and Practice

Although action learning articles have, over the years, appeared in many journals, the *"house journal"* for action learning is Action Learning: Research and Practice. Established in 2004, it seeks to publish material which advances knowledge and assists the development of the practice of action learning. Articles in the journal are intended to create theory which is grounded in empirical observation of data and experience that widens the understanding of action learning and research in professional and organisational settings. Published papers aim to encourage practitioners to gain new insights into their work and to help them improve their effectiveness and contribution to their clients and to the wider community. Contributors are asked to hold thinking and doing, theory and practice together. A key question for published papers is *"Is this likely to help people in the further development of their practice in working with people, organisations and communities?"* There are two types of papers:

Refereed Papers

These aim to combine theory and practice, to focus on processes and to seek to improve the impact of action learning, as well as conceptual papers addressing possible future development.

Accounts of Practice

These are stories telling of experience in using action learning and the consequent insights gained for self and organisation(s).

Three issues are published each year and further information is available at:

http://tandfonline.com/action/journalinformation?journalCod=calr20

The journal also organises an international action learning conference, held at various locations, every two years.

Further Reading

The ongoing development of action learning is expressed in many journal articles, book chapters, books and reports, so the following are only a sample of what is available.

Facilitating Action Learning: A Practitioner's Guide – M. Pedler and C. Abbott (2013) Maidenhead: Open University Press/McGraw-Hill – A useful guide for action learning facilitators which draws on extensive experience.

Action Learning for Managers – M. Pedler (2016) Abingdon: Routledge – A straightforward guide to action learning for managers well-illustrated with diagrams, checklists, questionnaires and case studies

Action Learning in Practice, 4th edition – M. Pedler (Ed.) (2011) Farnham: Gower Publishing – An exhaustive international compendium with contributions from many of the leading practitioners and which provides an authoritative overview of the theory and practice of action learning.

Action Learning: History and Evolution – Y. Boshyk and R. Dilworth (Eds.) (2010) Basingstoke: Palgrave Macmillan – The roots and evolution of action learning are the subject of this book.

Action Learning, Leadership and Organisational Development in Public Services – C. Rigg and S. Richards (Eds.) (2006) Abingdon: Routledge – A collection of accounts of action learning drawn from across a range of public services with an emphasis on leadership and the development of organisational capacity.

ABC of Action Learning – R. Revans (2011) Farnham: Gower Publishing – A clear and easy to read introduction to action learning.

The Origins and Growth of Action Learning – R. Revans (1982) Bromley: Chartwell-Bratt – Most likely out of print and so difficult to access, this is a collection of the early work of Reginald Revans, the founder of action learning comprising over 50 papers from the period 1945 to 1981.

Leading with Questions: How Leaders Discover Powerful Answers by Knowing How and What to Ask – M. Marquardt and B. Tiede (2023) Hoboken, NJ: John Wiley – A focus on asking questions that generate short- and long-term results and encourage participation, teamwork and creative thinking.

Revans Archive

In 1994 Revans gave most of his papers to Salford University and this comprises a rich and rewarding resource for Revans scholars. It contains unpublished papers on action learning and earlier versions of what was later published. It also provides insights into Revans the person and his family background. Alliance Manchester Business School also holds Revans-related material in hard copy form. Details of the archived material and how to access it are contained in the following:

Pedler, M., Edmonstone, J., Chambers, N. Mahon, A., Clark, E., Baxter, H., Mitchell, A. and Garlick, V. (2022) Action Learning: Resources Held in Manchester and Salford, Action Learning: Research & Practice, 19 (2): 120–129

International Foundation for Action Learning (IFAL)

Established in 1977 as the Action Learning Trust, it became IFAL in 1984 and is a registered educational charity in the UK. It is a non-profit organisation led by volunteers with an interest in the theory and practice of action learning. It maintains a library, a bibliographic service, provides an advisory service and runs events to promote discussions around action learning. It develops new programmes for members to learn with and from each other. Membership is open to individuals and organisations. Further information is available at www.ifal.org.uk

Institute of Leadership and Management (ILM)

The ILM is a registered UK charity and is a professional body offering accreditation for action learning facilitators. It endorses provision delivered by a range of bodies leading to a Certificate and Diploma in Action Learning Facilitation. Further information is at www.i-l-m.com

Global Forum on Leadership, Learning and Strategic Change

The Global Forum is a not-for-profit community of practice involving participants from major companies and organisations from around the world, who, in a collegiate spirit, discuss strategic change, executive learning and organisational development, commencing in 1996. Attendance at the annual Global Forum is by invitation only and is restricted to no more than 100 participants. Sessions take place over three and a half days in a range of different international locations. One of the objectives is to continually develop and improve methods and techniques in the business-driven action learning field, although the events are not confined to that purpose. Further information is available at www.globalforum-actionlearning.com

World Institute for Action Learning (WIAL)

The WIAL is a not-for-profit organisation dedicated to the advancement of a particular *"brand"* of action learning, associated with the work and writings of Professor Michael Marquardt, and within business and all community sectors. It works, often through affiliates, in many multinational private sector organisations, but also in some parts of the public sector. In this version the action learning set facilitator takes on the role of coach. WIAL makes claim to be the world's leading certifying body for action learning providing training and certification programmes internationally. More information is at www.wial.org

Action Learning, Action Research Association (ALARA)

Originating in Australia and largely southern hemisphere based, ALARA describes itself as a global network of programmes, institutions, professionals and people interested in using action learning and action research to generate collaborative learning, training, research and action to advance social change and to transform workplaces, schools, colleges, universities, communities, voluntary organisations, governments and businesses. Its vision is that action learning and action research will be widely used and publicly shared by individuals and groups creating local and global change for the achievement of a more equitable, just, joyful, productive, peaceful and sustainable society. It aims to facilitate networking amongst members and others in projects, research, teaching or learning about action learning, action research, process management and related approaches. Further information is available at www. alarassociation.org

Resource Tools

Three different sets of resource tools are described here. The first group are personal exercises which can be worked on by individual action learning set members. The second set are useful for reviewing the set's processes and progress and so are helpful for formative evaluation purposes. The third group are ways of using the ongoing dynamic of the set itself. All tools are considered under the headings of:

> *What is it?*
> *Why would I use it?*
> *When would I use it?*
> *How would I use it?*

Personal Exercises for Individual Set Members

These exercises are especially meaningful for people in mid-career, contemplating a career or life change and who wish to take stock to move on. It should always be voluntary whether set members decide to undertake work involving these exercises.

- ■ *Core process exercise*
  What is it? It is a form of biography work.
  Why should I use it? It offers a way for people to review their life in ways that transcend the narrow and ahistorical snapshots that many analytical approaches use. It results in an enriched perspective bringing both past and possible alternative futures together with the present for the purposes of understanding and action.
  When would I use it? To support individuals seeking to place job or career problems in an overall life context.
  How would I use it? Ask the set member to:
  - Divide their life into four or five sections, from birth to the present day.
  - Recall those moments, the feelings, sensations and experiences which were really fulfilling and motivating – of feeling at one with oneself and the world.

- Identify the special qualities, important patterns and themes around at the times of these moments.
- From this activity, identify the corer process or processes that have run through life and career, and which should be translated into the future.

■ *Life goals exercise*

What is it? A form of biography work.

Why should I use it? It offers a way for individuals to review their life resulting in an enlarged perspective bringing the past and potential futures together with the present to aid understanding and action.

When would I use it? To support people aiming to place job and career issues in a whole life context.

How would I use it? Ask the set member to:

- Draw an individual lifeline where one dimension (horizontal) is the passage of time from birth to the present and the other (vertical) relates to feelings of self-esteem, ranging from high to low.
- Prepare a life inventory of important personal happenings, including any peak experiences that can be identified; things that you do well; things that you do poorly; things you would like to stop doing; things that you would like to do well; peak experiences you would like to have; values that you want to live and things that you would like to start doing now.

Reviewing Set Processes

These exercises all help the set and its members to review how they are interacting together and hence provide feedback for improvement and for steering purposes.

■ *Action learning levels exercise*

What is it? A means of set members assessing their experience of the set.

Why should I use it? To discover where set members feel the focus of the set's working has been.

When would I use it? After a set meeting or at the end of a set's life.

How would I use it? Ask the set members, in reviewing the work of the set, if they had 100 points to distribute between the levels, where would they place these to show where the major focus of the set lay?

- Level 1: Problem-solving in relation to a specific issue.
- Level 2: Level 1, plus reframing of the issue and a conscious transfer of skills.

- Level 3: Levels 1 and 2, plus self-insight into personal processes of learning and other aspects of personal development.
- Level 4: Levels 1, 2 and 3, plus a focus on organisational culture and life/career issues.

▪ *Action learning problem brief*

What is it? A simple set of questions which will help a set member to think through a suitable issue for working on.

Why should I use it? To ensure that, prior to attending the first set meeting, a set member has carefully thought through the situation they are addressing.

When would I use it? Before the first set meeting.

How would I use it? By asking the set member to consider the following questions:

- Can you describe the issue you want to address in a single sentence?
- Why is this important to you? And to your organisation?
- What have you already tried that hasn't worked so far?
- How will you recognise progress on this issue?
- Who else would like to see progress on this issue?
- What difficulties do you anticipate?
- What are the benefits if this issue is resolved or reduced – to you? to other people? to the organisation?

▪ *Action learning set contract*

What is it? A statement of the responsibilities of the stakeholders associated with an action learning set.

Why would I use it? To ensure clarity of expectation between the major players.

When would I use it? Prior to, or shortly after, the first set meeting.

How would I use it? The contract ensures that there no confusion or ambiguity over who is responsible for what by setting out the responsibilities of everyone concerned. It is a template subject to modification or addition to suit local circumstances.

Set member

- To work with the sponsor to identify and agree an appropriate issue to be worked on at and between set meetings, accepting that it may evolve as the set progresses.
- To attend regularly set meetings and support and challenge fellow set members.
- To listen attentively to other set members.
- To follow-up action agreed at set meetings back in the workplace and report back at subsequent set meetings.

- To respect confidentiality and individual differences.
- To take part in evaluation and review.

Sponsor

- To identify people for whom involvement in an action learning
- set would be a useful development opportunity from the viewpoint
- of both the individual and the organisation.
- To become well-informed about the purpose and process of action learning and the work of the sponsored set member.
- To work with the set member to identify an appropriate issue, accepting that this may evolve as the set develops.
- To ensure the regular attendance of the set member at set meetings.
- To assist the set member with implementation of workplace actions emerging from set meetings.
- To take part in evaluation and review.

Facilitator

- To model appropriate behaviour for the set membership, including listening skills and useful questions.
- To be active in the early life of the set to foster a sense of collective identity and mutual interdependence.
- To be timely and appropriate in interventions, concentrating on the process to enable individual and group learning.
- To encourage set members to focus on agreed actions.
- To take part in evaluation and review.

■ *Action/reflection map*

What is it? A process to encourage set members to balance action and reflection in the set, accepting that this may differ for different set members.

Why would I use it? To reveal that the requisite balance between action and reflection will vary between set members, so that more or less reflection or action may be engendered for each person.

When would I use it? As part of a review at the end of a set meeting.

How would I use it? Each set member is asked to say how they felt the emphasis had been on taking action in the workplace during the set meeting on a scale of 0 (No emphasis) to 10 (Complete emphasis). Then they are asked to say how they felt the emphasis had been on reflection and review during the meeting on a similar scale. The score for each set member is plotted on a flipchart or wallchart graph with two axes – one for Action and the other for Reflection, ranging from 0 to 10 on each axis. This shows how individual set members experienced the set meeting and can stimulate discussion about the needed balance in future.

■ *Appreciative introductions*
What is it? A process for introducing set members to each other and start fostering a positive climate in a newly formed set.
Why would I use it? To address the anxiety and apprehension likely to be present at a first set meeting, establish a positive beginning and effect introductions.
When would I use it? At the first set meeting.
How would I use it? Set members are asked to pair up and share answers to such questions as
• Things I appreciate about working in my organisation.
• Things I appreciate about working on or addressing this issue.
• Things I appreciate about being part of this group.
• Things I appreciate about myself.
    Each partner has about 12 minutes to explore these, so around 15 minutes in total. Each individual then in turn introduced their partner to the set reporting what the partner said in response to the questions and adding "What I appreciate about the conversation we just had".
■ *Learning log*
What is it? A means of structuring report-backs to set meetings on action taken in the workplace.
Why would I use it? To ensure that workplace activities are reviewed in preparation for describing these to other set members.
When would I use it? Before a set meeting to get thoughts in order.
How would I use it? By seeking responses to the following questions:
• What was it I planned to do after the last set meeting?
• How did I go about it? What actions did I take?
• What were the responses to those actions?
• What were the outcomes or consequences?
• Was it what I anticipated? If yes, what went well? If no, what could I have done differently?
• What was I thinking?
• What was I feeling? Did my feelings match my actions?
• Did I do what I planned to do? If not, what was stopping me? What did I choose not to say or do and why did I make that choice?
• What do I want to focus on next time?
■ *Set meeting review worksheet*
What is it? A means of reviewing a set meeting, capturing the learning and emphasising the importance of follow-up action in the workplace.
Why would I use it? To give some shape to the set meeting review process, balancing personal insights with the need for progress in the workplace.

When would I use it? At the close of a set meeting.

How would I use it? At the end of a set meeting all set members spend about five minutes reflecting privately on the set's work before sharing the results with other set members. The reflection should focus on:

- *My issue* – the three things I've learned about my issue today are ... ...?
- *Me* – The one thing I've learned about myself today is ...?
- *Action* – My action steps before the next meeting are ...?
- *Other set members* – The most interesting things I've learned today about the issues facing the other set members are ...?

■ *Support/challenge map*

What is it? A process to help set members get the balance of support and challenge right for them, accepting that this may well differ for different set members.

Why would I use it? To reveal that the balance between support and challenge varies across set members.

Why would I use it? As part of a review at the close of a set meeting

How would I use it? Each set member is asked to say how they felt they had been supported in the set meeting on a scale of 0 (Not supported) to 10 (Totally supported). They are also asked to say how they felt they had been challenged in the meeting on a similar scale of 0 (Not challenged) to 10 (Fully challenged). The scores for each set member are plotted on a flipchart or wallchart graph with two axes – one for Support and the other for Challenge, ranging from 0 to 10 on each axis. This shows how individual set members experienced the meeting and can stimulate discussion about the degree of support and challenge needed in future set meetings.

Exercises Using the Set's Dynamics

These exercises employ the dynamic of the set to illustrate specific aspects of set membership and the learning that can be derived from it.

■ *Action learning constellations*

What is it? An exercise to help set members visualise how close or distant work relationships are and envisage a better alternative.

Why would I use it? To illustrate, in a spatial sense, the closeness or distance of work relationships.

When would I use it? When a set member describes a seemingly intractable work-based inter-relationship problem.

How would I use it?

- The set member presenting the issue describes the context, the stakeholders involved and the inter-relationship challenges.

- When completed the set member "places" the other set members around the room in a constellation to represent the positions that the stakeholders currently occupy at that stage of the issue. Some will be close to the set member and others further apart. Some will be looking at the issue and others looking away.
- In turn, these *"proxy stakeholders"* describe how it feels to be so positioned.
- The presenting set member then moves the proxy stakeholders to the position they feel would be most helpful in helping to address the issue.
- Again, the proxy stakeholders describe how the new positions feel.
- The presenting set member considers the implications of the movements in the room and how they might make them for real back in the workplace.

■ **Break-space exercise**

What is it? An exercise designed to jump-start the reflection process in the set.

Why would I use it? To encourage a reflective frame of mind at the start of a set meeting or when tension surfaces within the set.

When would I use it? Either at the start of a set meeting or when matters become pressurised in the set. In the latter case, reflection can relieve the stress level and provide reinforcement about the set's purpose.

How would I use it? The facilitator suggests set members take about 10 minutes at the start of each set meeting where all set members close their eyes, remain silent and reflect. Reflection can be general or focused. Some set members may feel that this is a distraction from a focus on their issue, but this is probably also attributable to awkwardness about being asked to reflect.

■ **Listening in the corner exercise**

What is it? An exercise enabling set members to practice reflecting on a situation by stepping away from it and looking at how others tackle it.

Why would I use it? When only one or two set members are in the spotlight during a set meeting.

When would I use it? When there's little evidence of listening behaviour in the set or when set members have difficulty in avoiding the "expert" role.

How would I use it? (All timings are indicative only)

- The set member with the issue they are struggling with describes it to the others. The others listen, do not interrupt but take notes about what comes to mind as they listen, focusing particularly on what might lie beneath the story being told and what it evokes in respect of their own feelings and associations (15 minutes).
- The other set members quickly rehearse their immediate thoughts and feelings. The set member with the issue stays silent while the others are

speaking, but has the opportunity, when they have finished, to return to anything they believe to be significant, without defence or correction. Questions for clarification can also be asked at this point, provided they are not leading questions designed to suggest a solution (15 minutes).

- The set member with the issue is invited to move out of the group away from the others and to sit in the corner, within earshot, but out of eyeshot. They are free to take notes on what they hear and think about what happens. The other set members discuss the issue and the presenter's involvement in it, as if they were not even in the room. The intention is that they use the opportunity to explore what is going on and reflect on their thoughts and feelings about the issue (30 minutes).

- The presenter re-joins the group and may pick up on certain points, ask for more information, rehearse what might happen if some proposals were initiated, and so on. They might also comment on what aspects of the discussion they overheard were most interesting, thought-provoking and helpful; what they found most challenging and difficult; what new insights might have been generated and what they intend to do next (15 minutes).

■ *Miracle question*

What is it? A way to help a set member describe their preferred future.

Why would I use it? When a set member seems lost in the intricacies of their situation with no obvious way out.

When would I use it? When a set member has difficulty in expressing exactly what a desirable future state might look like.

How would I use it? The facilitator says to the set member "Suppose you went to bed tonight, and a miracle happened. You have absolutely no idea how it occurred, but it just did. When you wake up in the morning the issue you've brought here to the set has gone". "What will you notice that tells you that the miracle has occurred?" "What else?" (Repeat this question five times) "Who else will notice?" "What will they notice?" (Repeat this five times)

■ *Pre-mortem*

What is it? An exercise for use when a set member is setting off on an initiative, so that it can be improved at the outset.

Why would I use it? To build in at an early stage attention to the possible pitfalls in taking forward a change.

When would I use it? When a set member is launching out on a new development.

How would I use it? The focal set member briefs the other set members on the proposed issue. They then tell the other set members, projected into the future, that the initiative has failed spectacularly. The set members then take time to try to think up and record every possible reason why it failed and then take it in turn to share items from their list. The whole set then seeks to *"re-design"* the initiative to accident-proof it against all possible sources of failure.

■ **Shuffled cards**

What is it? An exercise designed to provide feedback anonymously to set members to enhance trust and safety.

Why would I use it? To foster a sense of safety and security in the set.

When would I use it? Early in the life of the set – possibly at the first meeting.

How would I use it? The facilitator hands three small blank filing cards times the number of set members plus themselves to each person and asks them to record on each of the three cards on positive thing – a word or a short phrase – about each person in the set. On the other side of each card set members are asked to write the name of the person the attribute applies to. The cards are not signed by the members. The cards are placed in the centre of the set meeting, name side up and shuffled. Each person in the set is then given their cards name-side up. Each set member may then say how they feel if they wish to, but not to ask who wrote what.

■ **Slow-motion questioning exercise**

What is it? An activity done with a large group of people.

Why would I use it? To emphasise the importance of thinking about and delivering powerful questions and getting feedback on those that are most helpful.

When would I use it? As part of a taster or starter session to give people a flavour of action learning.

How would I use it?

- Working with a large group of people (around 20) who are interested in learning more about action learning, they are asked to work in groups of about five or six people. Chairs and tables are positioned so that everyone can see everyone else. Blank filing cards are issued to everyone.

- Everyone in the large group is asked to identify a current real difficult and challenging issue which they face and on which they would value some help. They write down the issue on one side of the card.

- A volunteer is sought from each group to describe and elaborate their issues a little to the other small group members for a few minutes to give them some background. If the volunteer describes a *"general"* issue the facilitator needs to get them to take personal responsibility for it, perhaps by phrasing it as "How can I …?" The other small group members turn their cards over, put their issues out of their minds, listen carefully to the volunteer and do not interrupt.

- Small group members do not comment at this stage. Instead, they listen and write down a powerful question that they would like to ask the volunteer on the blank side of their card. The question should be one that would help the volunteer to explore their issue and increase their understanding. Only questions are allowed – no comments.

- In turn, each member of the small group asks their question. They must be real questions – not advice-giving. The volunteer does not try to respond to these questions but instead listens and makes notes of each question, starring those with the greatest impact.

- When each small group member has asked their question, the volunteer chooses the two or three with the greatest impact which they think will be most useful in finding a way forward, or alternatively, those that were most interesting or intriguing.

- The volunteer reads out those two or three questions and says exactly why they were important. They might also address which questions they found most difficult; those they found most helpful; those that they can and cannot answer now.

- This provides useful feedback to the other group members on the relevance and utility of their questions.

- The larger group then reviews the nature and range of the questions posed and whether they were open or closed, together with what the major themes emerging from them were. This can expand into a discussion on the quality of good questions.

- ■ **SQIFED**
  What is it? A reflection model for use by set members.
  Why would I use it? To encourage deeper reflection.
  When would I use it? After a set member has had their airtime, to deepen their reflection on their issue.
  How would I use it? By encouraging the set member to ask:
  - *S* – What was my situation?
  - *Q* – What was the question that I addressed?
  - *I* – What insightful questions were asked of me by set members?
  - *F* – What is now my focus of reflection?
  - *E* – What is the nature of my further exploration of this?
  - *D* – What development pointers arise for me now?

- ■ *Thinking, feeling and willing to exercise*
  What is it? An approach focusing on the three major questions central to action learning. They are "Who knows?" (thinking), "Who cares?" (feeling) and "Who can?" (willing).

Why would I use it? To avoid over-intellectualising approaches to issues by set members.

When would I use it? When a large group of people are ready to form into action learning sets, as a means of highlighting the key questions.

How would I use it? The facilitator splits a large group into smaller groups with four people in each. One person talks for 10–15 minutes about an issue important to them. The remaining three people listen without interruption or asking questions – just paying attention to what the first person is saying, with one each of the three concentrating on:

- Thinking: What is being said by the first person – the thought patterns. Is it logical? Detailed or general? Focusing on the past, present or future? Who is being talked about and who is not? What images and metaphors are being used? What assumptions are being made?
- Feeling: What does the speaker seem to be feeling? Consider gestures, posture, tone of voice, way of breathing, facial expressions and eye movements.
- Willing: What does the person want to do? A wish or a dream or a real intention to act?

The three listeners report back what they have each heard and seen from the thinking, feeling and willing viewpoints to the first person, who needs to consider how this fits with their own perceptions. This can be repeated so that all four people have the same opportunity.

Trauma, Trivia and Joy

What is it? An exercise for dealing with the natural anxiety of new set members to allay their concerns and help with formation of the set.

Why would I use it? To help new members relax and convey how they are feeling with an informal immediacy.

When would I use it? At an initial set meeting.

How would I use it? Each person in the set is asked to describe briefly an event or incident that has happened to them recently, one of which could be described as a trauma, another as a trivia and a third as a joy. Each set member describes their events. There is no discussion of the events, although set members may convey feelings and empathy non-verbally, creating a warm and supportive atmosphere to relax each other and get to know each other a little. This takes between 5 and 15 minutes, depending on the contributions made.

Index

Printed in the United States
by Baker & Taylor Publisher Services